Learn the
Secret Ingredient
to Attract,
Influence,
Deeply Connect
and get the
Success
you always
wanted

Praise for 'The Attention Switch'

Attention Switch is a unique and fresh approach to changing your life for once and for all, and getting ahead. Make sure you get into action and actually implement this great advice. Highly recommended!

Ron G Holland - Top Biz Guru and Author of 'Talk & Grow Rich' and 'The Eureka! Enigma'

A very timely and powerful message that everyone can benefit from

Barry Philips - Managing Director Knowledge is King

In 'The Attention Switch' Itzik has hit on the one thing that so many businesses forget - giving 'Authentic Attention' rather than just lip service. His passion for the subject shines through on every page and he truly practices what he preaches.

Deri Llewellyn Davies - 'The Strategy Man' author of 'Strategy on a Page'

&& Dale Carnegie super upgraded
for the cyber age! **""**

**Professor Paul Moorcraft
- international speaker and author**

&& There is no doubt that Authentic Attention **""**
can transform relationships in business and
in life. Itzik Amiel, in his very readable and
comprehensive book, give us the tools and
strategies to dramatically transform our
success. No wonder this is the networking
book the world is talking about!

**Ben Kench - author of
'Selling for Dummies' and
'More Money, Less Stress'**

"If you have contacts
you DO NOT need money:
Start PAYING ATTENTION -
the new and real currency."

Itzik Amiel

"I'd like to offer you a special gift!"

If you would like to take the ideas and strategies in 'The Attention Switch' to the next level, then go to the link below and join me to receive further insights, case studies, news, and advance information on Attention Switch events around the world.

www.AttentionSwitch.com/gift

Meet the author

Itzik Amiel [attorney-at-law] is the Global Leading Authority on Attention Networking™ and Relationship Capital; Author; International Professional Speaker; Power Networker; Founder & CEO, EyeRon Group [International Expansion Group] and Power Networking Academy.

An award-winning professional and highly sought after keynote speaker, leading international power networker and international expansion and business development expert. Itzik Amiel is a rare find.

Itzik has extensive experience gained as an international tax lawyer and throughout executive international business development roles in a global financial institution and leading professional firms and trust companies. Itzik has successfully assisted clients develop new business and realize a substantial growth and rapid expansion. His clients ranging from Fortune/ FTSE 1000 corporations, middle market privately held companies to professional associations. Itzik is also founder of global professional networks and communities and a partner and global expansion director of one the leading global professional networks.

As a bespoke speaker and trainer, Itzik has dedicated using Authentic Attention™ tools to help:

►Leaders persuade and influence others with confidence and purpose;

►Companies stand out from their rivals and attract clients and expand to new markets;

►Organisations engage and motivate their employees;

►People will enhance their networking skills by using Attentional Networking™

Itzik's clients have includes many large companies and SMEs as well as thousands of executives and entrepreneurs from around the globe who attend his presentations and seminars.

Itzik's famous seminars and events include 'The Power Networking Academy' and 'Attentional Networking'.

Meet Itzik and don't miss Itzik's ongoing secrets to networking and building relationships.

Find out more at
www.ItzikAmiel.com

For the four important ladies in my life.

I dedicate this book to the loving memory
of my beloved mother, Ruth Amiel.
I will never forget you mom!

I also dedicate this book to the jewel of my life,
my dear wife and best friend, Mariska Amiel,
who brings so much love and joy into my life,
I am truly blessed.

And for my loving daughters, Noa and Zoe.
You are the treasures of my life,
the source of
authentic attention,
wisdom and love.
I love you!

"To expand
globally,
start by
expanding
your own
horizons."

Itzik Amiel

THE ATTENTION SWITCH™

HOW TO PAY WITH THIS SECRET INGREDIENT TO ATTRACT, INFLUENCE, DEEPLY CONNECT & GET THE SUCCESS YOU ALWAYS WANTED

ITZIK AMIEL

www.itzikamiel.com

Published by
Filament Publishing Ltd
16, Croydon Road, Waddon, Croydon,
Surrey, CRO 4PA, United Kingdom
Telephone +44 (0)20 8688 2598
Fax +44 (0)20 7183 7186
info@filamentpublishing.com
www.filamentpublishing.com

ISBN 978-1-910125-15-1
Printed by CreateSpace

www.ItzikAmiel.com
www.AttentionSwitch.com

Contents

"Attentional Networking
is the art of
being you."

Itzik Amiel

ACKNOWLEDGEMENTS

This book could not have been written without the help and encouragement of many family members, friends, customers, partners and other great attentional networkers. They helped in so many ways: through advice, positive criticism, and professional suggestions and recommendations. I give heartfelt thanks for their generous support and cooperation. I am grateful for the time you took to help me.

My biggest thanks and appreciation go to my dear wife, Mariska Amiel, the love of my life and my first point of attention. No words can adequately express the feelings and gratitude I have for her. She has done and is still doing so very very much for me and our family and has given up herself to give her authentic attention to others each and every day. More than anyone else in my life, she gives me her sincere attention whenever I ask for it, with dedication and love. She has challenged me on every detail and made me reach and grow both personally and professionally. Thank you my dear and my best friend!

I owe particular gratitude to our two daughters, Noa and Zoe. Every day you bring new light into my life and teach me to understand what true attention is all about. In the limited edition of this book, I promise to include a chapter on 'paying attention to your family'. It'll be filled with the lessons that you taught me. Thank you for your valuable suggestions, insightful advice and enthusiasm.

I can never sufficiently thank my beloved mother, Ruth Amiel, the original attention giver. I miss you every day. With her big smile and positive attitude, she gave me the power to care about other people and to connect with them authentically. She taught me so many of the lessons and values that I've implemented in my life and in writing this book. She taught me to be proud of who I am.

I also want to thank my dad, Moshe Amiel, for investing in us and believing that a good education and personality are the most important components for a good life. Dad, I am sure you are proud of us for all our achievements and the importance we place on helping others and giving them our authentic attention.

The list wouldn't be complete without thanking my dear aunts, Ettie and Yael. Thank you for your wisdom, care, love and empathy for me and my four dear sisters. You have been like mothers to me, always spoiling me and reminding me never to give up. I am proud to be part of a family that emphasizes the importance of giving to others.

Many thanks to my publisher, for his enthusiasm, wise advice and for making this book a valuable asset and a leading guide to motivation and networking. And for my friends and business partners who believed in the Attention Switch™ networking philosophy from the very beginning. They helped me create valuable frameworks that made my vision clearer and more approachable. Plus all my international friends – I want to thank you from the bottom of my heart for your invaluable input and support.

And obviously, to all you wonderful customers, clients, partners and friends who encouraged me to write down my knowledge and patiently waited until this book was ready – thank you very much! I've practiced my attention giving skills with many of you over the years. I will never ever forget that without you, my greatest living testimonials, I would never have succeeded.

"This is one of the most basic facts of human psychology. We are flattered by other people's attention. It makes us feel special. We want to be around people who show interest in us. We want to keep them close. And we tend to reciprocate their interest by showing interest in them."

Dale Carnegie

INTRODUCTION

A wise teacher once gave his young protégé a riddle to solve:

"You possess a very powerful tool — one that is always with you.
You can use this tool at any time to make decisions more efficiently,
to make interactions with others more rewarding
and to find more joy in life.
What is this amazing tool?"

Perhaps the following story will give you the answer.

The hug of my life

"Hugging is a big thing for me". I say this almost every time I'm on stage, but I never go into any more detail. For years it was a secret between my wife and I, later I only shared it with a very small group of people. But the time has come to share it with you too my dear friend.

A hug is one of the many ways you can show another person sincere attention and caring. A hug can help you bond with another person in just a few seconds. But in my case one very special hug saved my life.

It happened back in the days when we lived in Israel, when we were still just boyfriend and girlfriend. My girlfriend lived and worked in Jerusalem and I worked in Tel Aviv. I visited her a few times each week leaving early the next morning to take bus number 18 to the central station in

Jerusalem. From there I would catch an intercity bus to Tel Aviv. It was the same routine every time, with the same people waiting in the station each morning, boarding the same bus, and sitting on the same seats as if they had reserved them. A normal morning routine.

It was just another day. I woke up full of energy, rushed my coffee and breakfast and was about to leave my girlfriend's house to get the bus. This morning my lovely girlfriend wanted to give me a warm, deep hug, so I sank into her arms for a few seconds before dashing out to catch the bus. Arriving on the corner of the street, I realized that the bus was already leaving the station. Sh... I'd have to wait for the next one.

Ten minutes later the next bus arrived and I was soon on my way to the central station. I felt relaxed but a little sad too. I didn't know why at the time.

Early into the journey the police stopped the bus and asked it to change its route since the main road was blocked. The bus driver tried to find out what had happened. The only thing the policeman shared was that there had been a terrorist attack 10 minutes earlier. The bus driver turned on his radio to listen to the breaking news. As I listened in I went cold with shock... I heard that the terrorist attack had targeted bus number 18... Yes, the same bus I took every morning and had missed that day... There were no survivors. All the passengers had been killed.

I began to realize that my life was a gift. I understood that the long hug from my girlfriend had saved my life. Without it I would have been one of the poor souls on bus number 18.

I was a few hours late for work that day. I was in a state of absolute shock and so full of sadness... An hour later I received a call from a lady I'd known five years before. We hadn't kept in touch and I don't know to this day why she called or how she found my number.

"Are you okay Itzik?" she asked. It was strange: there were many terrorist attacks in Jerusalem and she'd never called me before. She didn't call again either. She called just that one time. Was somebody trying to send me a message?

The next day the newspapers were full of the victims' photographs. I knew most of their faces. These were the people who'd shared the same journey with me day after day. Now they were gone and I was still alive in this world.

That day changed my life. It changed me. From that day onward, hugs have become infinitely precious. Every time somebody hugs me sincerely something deep inside of me is touched. I'm reminded of that day in Jerusalem; the day I got a second chance.

My girlfriend became my wonderful wife and hugs continue to be a great way for us to give authentic attention to each other and to other people. And that special hug? This was the moment when I first understood the awesome power of Authentic Attention™. I began to think about it as a concept and tool. Real sincere attention is of profound importance in everyone's life. In my personal case – it literally saved my life!

What was the powerful tool that the teacher gave his young protégé?

The ability to use and give your attention to the people and things you decide to give it to! In this book I will explain why this tool is so powerful.

You can use it at any time to make decisions more efficiently, to deepen your connection with others, and to find more joy in your life.

Why this book?

Building relationships with other people will always be part of our lives in one form or another. The need to connect to others applies to people everywhere, no matter who you are, where you live, or what you do for a living.

You may be surprised and encouraged to learn that while an inability to connect with others may look and feel like a communication problem, in most cases it isn't. I believe it is primarily an educational problem.

This conviction has grown out of my own experiences. For years I looked for a powerful tool that would help me train my mind so it would be easy to use, did not depend on special skills and help me live a rich and fulfilling life, while building long-lasting relationships with others.

The life-saving incident was that special moment for me. At that moment I knew I was not going to let negative people steal the best of me. I'd survived to share my gift with others. I started to see myself as someone who had purpose. Thus, my odyssey began.

At this point I began to notice that many people struggled with connecting and networking, while I had finally learned to cope and push through obstacles. How could I help these people? How can I help you?

I decided to write about ATTENTION because although it's a valuable concept, many people are unaware of it. I have a deep desire to share the answers I've discovered about building relationships and connecting with others.

These days it is especially important to understand the concept of ATTENTION giving. Today we have more scientific tools and insights into the world and ourselves than ever, yet our ability to give attention – especially to other human beings – is under siege. Our children are being distracted more than any generation in human history.

We are living at a time of increasing new technologies, new instruments, and new developments. It's no wonder that we are constantly distracted and find it difficult to give our full attention to one person.

Yet improving your attention skills is the secret ingredient to success in every aspect of your life. Not only this, but it helps change your perspective so that you see the world as a less threatening and more joyous place.

People around me, my friends, family members, and students, were amazed at how shifting their thinking about networking and relationship-building magically reshaped their lives. As I listened to them and learned from their wisdom, these same people helped me reaffirm and add to my fund of knowledge about attention-giving

I learned that ATTENTION is not just one thing. Attention has many varieties. Each kind of attention is important at the right time in the right place. Every person can learn how to switch between different levels of Attention.

- **CONCENTRATED ATTENTION** is when we pay full attention. Concentration means being able to focus on one thing and ignore anything outside it.

- **CURRENT ATTENTION**. This is just being with the person or task that is right in front of you, paying full current attention in the moment to the people around you. This is different to concentrated attention as it calls for a more panoramic style of awareness.

- **RANDOM ATTENTION**. This is very different from the first two. It means letting your mind go wherever it wants and it is essential for creativity and innovation.

  A word of warning:
  if you're using Random Attention while dealing with other people, they may believe that you're not giving them authentic attention (since your mind is roaming wherever it wants). So be discerning about how and when you use it because it could reflect negatively on your ability to build authentic relationships with others.

It's important to understand what kind of attention is needed at any given time, especially with regards to other people. The data tells us that the ability to pay attention well – to the right people, in the right way, in the right place, at the right time – is absolutely critical to peak personal (and collateral) performance. If you wish to succeed in life you have to pay attention.

How this book can work miracles in your life

I assume that you, like most of us, wonder what the secrets of success may be. You know that if you could only get your hands on these secrets then there's no reason why you couldn't be successful too. But you can't find these secrets as part of any higher education course. And there are few books out there because these secrets are rarely addressed by specialists.

You have a lot of questions. How do other people create lives that are filled with achievement? How can you turn an acquaintance into a real friend? Why does one person have to spend a lot of time connecting with others, while another immediately connects with every person she meets? How do you meet people who can help you advance in life?

How come some people go to an event or conference and almost instantaneously develop great connections with strangers that, weeks or months later, turn into a deal or a potential new client?

Where are the answers to these questions? Right here. My book answers every one of them.

In this book, I will explain and share ideas and methods I have practiced for many years. They've brought me great success and a life of unrestrained enthusiasm and joy. I will share with you the solutions that ultimately led me to special opportunities, connected me with powerful and accomplished people and which helped me achieve a lot of success in my personal as well as my professional life. Implement the ideas in this book and you will connect with authentic attention™ with other people. And you'll become a powerful networker too. This book will enable you to build sincere relationships with others; ones that will help you create a successful life and achieve fantastic results very fast.

But it'll take a lot of work and dedication. You need to really think and care about other people, not just yourself. The ultimate result will be that these same people will be there for you to help you accomplish your life goals. This sincere attention will draw together a strong network of people who you care for and who care for you. You'll help each other to live much fuller, happier and richer lives.

Many people around the world have asked me: "Why is it I have tried and tried to connect with other people but with no success?" In this book you will find the reasons for this common complaint.

I have no doubt that everybody can follow the simple and practical methods in this book.

Also you 'beginners' who are opening my book for the first time, trust me when I tell you that you too can quickly learn to connect with power, enthusiasm and care. That's what this book is all about.

It takes a lot of reinforcement to incorporate new concepts of relationship-building into your daily routine and behaviour, so please commit to following the advice in this book. I promise you that the more involved you are and the more you try, the more fun you will have. You will see great improvement in your communication and connections with others and you will be set on the royal road to deeply connecting with other people. Everybody has the capacity to become a great relationship builder.

You can master Authentic Attention™ with your friends, family members, co-workers or employees – even with strangers.

The concepts and tools you are about to discover in this book are meant to be part of your daily life and to serve you forever. Learn them well and you can conquer any relationship-building challenge. You will be absolutely amazed at the incredible amount of power you hold inside you.

You know deep inside that you have many wonderful abilities waiting to be discovered. Now is the perfect time to do so. You can begin to use the productive ideas in this book immediately, smoothing your daily interaction with others and bringing harmony to your relationships. I invite you to discover with me the secrets of AUTHENTIC ATTENTION™ – it's an exciting and rewarding journey.

"Be yourself;
everybody else
is already taken."

Oscar Wilde

PART ONE

The Power
of
Authentic Attention™

"CONTACTS
YOU SHARE,
YOU <u>DO NOT</u>
OWN

SHARING =
GIVING + HAPPINESS"

Itzik Amiel

CHAPTER 1

WHAT IS ATTENTION?

"Obtaining attention is obtaining
a kind of enduring wealth,
a form of wealth
that puts you
in a preferred position
to get anything
this new economy offers."

Michael H Goldhaber

CHAPTER 1: WHAT IS ATTENTION?

ATTENTION: DEFINITION

What is Attention?

I always knew that there was something different about my communication and interaction with other people. But despite constantly asking myself what it was, I had no idea! I knew it was nothing to do with my knowledge or my degrees: I definitely hadn't studied it. Maybe it was something to do with my personal character. Could it be genetic?

Over the years, this mysterious skill improved and I began to gain some insights into it. For example, I realized that although it wasn't just about my verbal or non-verbal (e.g. body language) communication with other people, it was definitely connected to it.

This is the thing I call 'Attention'. We all know it exists. Everyone can do it. But it's really hard to define. How do you define this feeling you give to another human being to express that you care about him/her? How do you define the look that silently says: 'yes, I see you. Thank you for being in my life'? How can I define attention in a way that everybody will understand?

Let's get to work, since I have a lot to share with you.

Here's Wikipedia's definition:

"Attention is the cognitive process of selectively concentrating on one aspect of the environment while ignoring other things. Attention has also been referred to as the allocation of processing resources."

Quite complicated isn't it? Attention is one of the most intensely studied topics within psychology and cognitive neuroscience. It'll be useful for you to hear some basic information about it so that you can then go on to use Attention to drive your own success.

According to John Ratey (2001), attention is much more than just noticing incoming stimuli. It involves a number of processes, including filtering out perceptions, balancing multiple perceptions and attaching emotional significance to these perceptions.

The truth is that no one can really define attention. Whatever it is, it is bound up in hard to grasp notions such as consciousness, awareness and focus. These confusing terms are the source of much debate in fields like philosophy, neuroscience and marketing. But I will plough ahead regardless. What follows combines insights from these various fields in a crude attempt to define attention-giving or — more specifically — what it means for one person to pay attention to another.

The six steps of the attention process

Attention is a process rather than a thing. It can be broken down into six steps.

• Step 1: Alertness
Alertness is the initial step in the attention process. If we are going to do something, or listen to someone, we need to feel alert, as though our battery is fully charged and our brains have enough energy. Just like our bodies need physical energy if we are going to run, our brains need mental energy if we are going to think.

• Step 2: Selectivity

The next step in the attention process is selectivity. Our attention can potentially be captured by a multitude of stimuli. We can't pay attention to everything – our conscious mind just couldn't handle it – so we must decide which stimuli are the most important. Attention has a very important role – it chooses what we are going to tune into.

Imagine yourself sitting at a seminar. What are you paying attention to? The other attendees? The slide on the board? Maybe to the colour of someone's tie? From these many possibilities, the brain must decide what is the most relevant information to focus on from moment to moment.

Now think about a task. There are often parts of it that need more focus than others. The ability to select the most important part of a task is called saliency determination. (A salient stimulus stands out from other stimuli). For example, go back to your imaginary seminar and look at the people around you; if they're all dressed in ordinary clothes with ordinary hairstyles, we probably wouldn't notice anyone in particular. But what if one of them was naked and had green hair? You'd probably remember him! He would be very salient to us.

• Step 3: Dealing with distractibility

Which stimuli should we choose at any given moment? How do we choose the most important stimuli? We have to filter out things that distract us if we want to accomplish anything. Distractions can be auditory or visual. They could come from our own bodies in the form of feelings or irrelevant thoughts. Do you remember the last time random thoughts distracted you from a task? And before you knew it, one thought led to another which led to another until your mind had wandered far away from the job in hand.

• Step 4: Duration of attention

Once we've chosen what to attend to and have filtered out any distractions, we must attend to it for the right amount of time – not too long, not too short. This is called duration of attention.

We need to have mental energy if we're going to think. But we must also maintain or sustain this mental energy for the time it takes to finish the job. Just as we need physical energy to start a race, we also need enough energy to finish the race. Our energy must be both consistent and sufficient.

• Step 5: Preview

The fifth component of the attention process is called previewing. Previewing can be thought of as reflection and planning. To do this, we must consider the consequences of each possible action and eliminate those that do not lead to the desired outcome. Failing to take the time to engage in necessary planning or previewing is called impulsivity or the inability to inhibit behaviour or to regulate behaviour by its consequences.

Think about the last time you did something. Did you consider all of the possible actions you could perform and decide which one to take before you began? Did you choose the best action given the set of circumstances you found yourself in?

Previewing is essential if you want to interact well with other people. For example, when you're talking to someone and their comments trigger something you want to say, you should wait until they've finished talking before saying it. Here's another example, think about the last time you took a multiple-choice test. If you want to do well, you must read all of the choices and think about each one before making your selection. Previewing skills help you pass multiple-choice exams!

• Step 6: Self-monitoring

I don't know about you, but it is normal for me to monitor and learn from every task I do. That includes checking over a task that is in progress, assessing the progress, and making adjustments when necessary. I believe that self-monitoring is the sixth component of attention. In short, self-monitoring is 'watching' ourselves doing something while we are doing it. Another way to put it is being aware of our awareness.

Many of us use this process and realize its importance when taking tests or preparing a presentation or paper. You want to be sure, in these situations, to monitor yourself so that you do not wander off the subject or make careless mistakes.

I trust you agree that in order to complete a task, not only must sufficient time (i.e. duration) be allotted to the task, but also the pace must be sufficient so that each relevant aspect of the task can be attended to. Self-monitoring should also include the speed of concentration or attention to a task. In addition, it involves the ability to predict how long a specific task will take.

For optimum self-monitoring, review the task at the beginning and put its components in order starting with the most difficult or most important parts and ending with the easiest or least important. The first on the list should be given more time than the one at the end. For example, more time should be set aside to prepare for an important meeting than to write a greeting card.

Knowing this six-step process may help you, my dear reader, understand what you need to do in your day-to-day life in order to pay authentic attention and get the success you've always wanted. This basic process will help us turn your switch to ON before diving into the real secrets of Attention.

ATTENTION TO WHAT?

Many people are proud of their ability to multitask. But I think they fail to appreciate a fundamental truth about Attention.

I remember one large international conference that was aimed at professionals. Instead of paying full attention to the presentation, many people were checking their Smartphones, texting, or emailing. So where was their attention? Not on the thing they'd paid money (and sometimes a lot of money) to participate in.

Attention deficit, it seems, has infected everyone in this 24/7 world.

In the course of researching this book I've read many of the papers written in the past decade about attention deficit. The research shows us how the brain focuses, what impairs that focus and how easily the brain can be distracted. The good news is that the brain can learn to ignore distractions, making you more focused, creative, and productive. We can learn how to pay attention to one thing, one person.

So how do you shift your attention to a specific thing? How can you start to improve your attention skills? Exactly how do you give 'undivided attention' to one person?

Control your 'out of control' state

Emotions are processed in the brain by the amygdala, which adversely responds to negative emotions such as anxiety, sadness or anger.

While negative emotions block the ability of the brain to solve problems and do other productive work, research shows that positive emotions have the opposite effect; their stimulus improves creative and strategic thinking.

So what does this teach us about developing attention skills? Emotions are clearly important, so work on improving your balance of positive and negative feelings. If, for example, someone irritates you, let it go. Accept the automatic reaction, take a few breaths, and let go of the irritation. Try charging up on positive emotions before going into meetings. They'll generate more positivity as well as improving your brain function (and that of others), leading to better teamwork and problem solving.

Stop with full power

Distractions are always lurking. Even when you are focused on a particular task, your brain continuously scans your internal and external environment. The good news is that the brain can stop a random thought instantly. Moreover, the brain can stop unnecessary actions and even instinctive emotions from getting you off track.

Knowing that, what can you do in order to improve your attention to a specific thing?

I recommend you use three steps:

- **Awareness**. Be aware of your options: to stop what you are doing and solve this distraction or to continue with what you are doing.
- **Consideration.** Take your time and consider the options.
- **Choose.** Stop or continue; it's as simple as that.

This three-step process is a simple and guaranteed way to control your attention. I use this method many times every day. It helps me ensure that my attention goes to the right things, the right people and the right tasks.

Give your brain a break

If it's time to shift your attention from one task to another, I recommend that you give your brain a break. Before you turn your attention to a new task, shift your focus from your mind to your body. Go for a run or a walk, or do some other physical activity. This is a great way to allow your brain to draw a line under previous tasks and create a clear space for a new one.

In my last company, I used to schedule physical breaks during meetings. It was amazing how often team members came up with innovative ideas during them. Some of the ideas were so good that we acted on them. Why not give yourself a break? Even a five minute break can make a big difference.

ATTENTION = THE NEW CURRENCY

'Attention Economy' (a concept originated in the mid-eighties by writer and consultant Michael H. Goldhaber) is rapidly becoming the dominant economy in which we live. It is fast replacing, not merely transforming, the old money-based economy. The English expression 'PAY attention' underlines the fact that attention is a sort of currency that's as real as money.

I know that Attention is a good substitute for real money. For example, the last time I flew from Las Vegas back to Amsterdam, I spent a little time talking to the ground stewardess. This simple act of attention won an immediate reward when she upgraded me to business class (an upgrade that cost a lot of money or many airline points).

What do you pay when you pay attention?

What is paying attention all about? Why should people pay attention to other people's actions or words? And why don't people pay more attention to attention?

One pays attention to another person's actions, expressions, emotions and thoughts. By paying attention to anyone, we activate certain chains of thought and memory in our own brains, and each time we do it, it becomes easier to activate not only similar processes but memories of that person. So the next time we encounter them we can easily recall previous interactions.

It's the nerve connections or neuron chains in your own brain that allow you to recognize what another person is doing or how they're feeling.

Say you see someone picking up a cup. If you observe them picking it up and drinking from it, one set of neurons fires; but if they put the dirty cup in the sink, a different chain of neurons is activated.

When we pay attention to another human being we temporarily align and reshape our mind to match their mind. Thus, you want what she wants, think her thoughts, and feel her feelings. If you don't then you are not really paying attention. Paying true attention is such a powerful act that your brain will remember it. This paves the way for easier and more natural exchanges between you and that same person in the future.

Haven't you ever noticed a stranger at some social event and wondered what they'd be like to talk to? Then, later on, the two of you find yourselves in the middle of a wonderful discussion. This is attention in action. Your brain flagged the stranger at the moment you first paid attention to them. So when you finally got into conversation, it felt easy and natural.

Attention wealth

"If you have contacts, you do not need money."

Itzik Amiel

A person who is wealthy in Attention is someone with the ability to give a large amount of Attention. Attention wealth is different from financial wealth – money is finite so we have to protect it by depositing it in the bank or setting up an investment portfolio. Attention wealth is a resource that can't be affected by the poor decisions of others, as monetary wealth has been in the recent banking crisis.

Attention Wealth is stored in the mind and memory bank, and memories persist. Thus, people can use their attention wealth in many ways which we will explain in more length later in the book.

The more people you pay attention to, the more they will want what you want, whether it's a personal objective or a desire to help the world in some way. This ability to pay attention to whoever whenever makes you an Attention wealthy person. Giving attention to others can guarantee you get whatever you want, and you don't necessarily have to convert that attention into money.

At the same time it's a fact that money tracks attention. If one gives enough attention one can earn quite a bit of money, while if one cannot give enough attention to other people (so attracting attention) one tends to earn less and less. There is definitely a direct relationship between giving attention to others and money-earning potential. Perhaps in future we may even reach a point where money as currency is simply no longer necessary.

The 'Attention Bank'

In his article 'The Economy of Attention' Georg Franck says: "What is more pleasant than the benevolent notice other people take of us, what is more agreeable than their compassionate empathy? What inspires us more than addressing ears flushed with excitement, what captivates us more than exercising our own power of fascination? What is more thrilling than an entire hall of expectant eyes, what more overwhelming than applause surging up to us? What, lastly, equals the enchantment sparked off by the delighted attention we receive from those who profoundly delight ourselves? Attention by other people is the most irresistible of drugs. To receive it outshines receiving any other kind of income. This is why glory surpasses power and why wealth is overshadowed by prominence."

No wonder I deeply believe that attention is the new currency! If we were to rank income in terms of attention rather than money, I'm definitely a wealthy man. What about you?

Can we save and invest the attention we receive from others as we can with money? It's a nice idea, everyone with their own attention bank account and using their attention savings to build more wealth in the form of new or better relationships.

But there is still a significant difference between attention income and money income. The value of attention income depends on who it comes from. As Gregor Franck says: "Attention coming from people we admire is most precious; it is valuable coming from those we esteem; it counts little coming from people towards whom we are indifferent; and attention may even assume a negative value coming from people we despise or fear."

THE ESSENTIAL INGREDIENT

One of the main things I've learned to do is to look into a person's eyes when I'm talking to them. It feels as though the eyes are windows to their past, present and future. When I look at another person, I look with all that I have. If you pay enough attention there is nothing that you will not be able to overcome.

How did this process begin? When I was young I realized that I didn't know anything and I wanted to know more. I believed that if I paid enough attention, I would one day know and learn everything I wanted. Over the years I used it for personal growth purposes, but in the last decade I noticed that 'Attention' was also very helpful in business and in creating authentic relationships. Knowing that you do not know is one of the greatest insights you will ever have. When you fully realize that you do not know anything, you will naturally begin to pay more attention.

Even in business, the only reason why one person seems to get all the opportunities is simply because they see them, while other people do not. Leaders have vision; they are able to see more clearly than others.

Over the years, I practiced 'Attention without Intention'. I was being generally attentive and not paying attention to something specific.

Although I wasn't focusing on any one thing, I still held to the intention to pay attention. I realized that when I focused on something or somebody, I could create just about anything. So I constantly focused on enhancing and sharpening my attention skills.

How do you know you exist? Could it be because of attention? When you fall asleep where does that attention go? Where is that awareness of your own existence? So the basis of your existence is attention! And this attention does not depend on anything except yourself. You can choose to hone your attention to a keen edge, as it will help you do anything you want to do.

Are you a human being or are you an historian? Are you interested in observing and recording the other people in your life or do you want to experience deep and satisfying relationships with them? If you really want to know somebody, you have to give them your authentic Attention. Otherwise your life will merely become a record of interactions with others. Wherever you go these days you'll see someone using their camera or Smartphone to capture the moment so they can share it with everybody online. They want to record everything; almost as though it's the only way they can prove to themselves that they actually met these people. Nothing else remains but the picture. Think of the last time you were blown away by an experience or interaction with another human being; do you need a picture to help you remember it?

THE ATTENTION SWITCH

It's important to me that you, my dear friend, thoroughly understand Attention. This understanding will serve you well when you start working with it to create the success you've always wanted. If I can do it so can you!

My research taught me another important lesson: many people mistakenly see Attention and awareness as the same thing. Wrong.

Attention and awareness are different. Let me explain. When we use the terms 'awareness' or 'level of awareness' we usually mean something like consciousness or perception. That's another way of saying that someone is alive! Awareness can only be turned off at the moment of death. It's always on, although the level of intensity can change.

On the other hand, Attention is just mental alertness. It is a mental state that you can turn on and off. You can close it down or open it up whenever you want. You can pay Attention to somebody or you can withdraw your attention from them. Since it is an act of attention of the mind, it exists only in the psychological dimension rather than the existential one.

Your Attention is like a Switch. You are in charge of turning it on or off. But let me explain it a bit more. I want you to be aware of your surroundings as you sit and read this book (I hope you're enjoying it so far!) Is there anyone with you? Are you alone? Are you in your own home or in a hotel room? Try to perceive everything that is around you with all your senses.

Let's assume you fall into a daydream – we all do it many times every day. Even though your senses still receive information about your surroundings, you do not perceive it as clearly in this state. Your mental alertness has stepped down a level compared to where it is right now. So, by simple logic, if your mental alertness can decrease, you can surely increase it too. Do you agree? If you consciously increase your alertness, your perception of reality, of other people, becomes clearer and clearer. This will intensify your physical experience of interactions with other people.

I am certain that whatever attention level you have right now is not all that is possible for you. There is far more, but you do not have access to it yet; it is still only a potential. But of one thing I am certain: you need to pay all the Attention you can in order to reap the rewards of this secret ingredient.

It's obvious that we move between different levels of attention at different times of the day. If you are working, you use a different level of attention than if you're watching TV. If you are doing something you like very much, your attention will be higher than when you're doing something that bores you. I can promise that whatever peak attention level you've reached before, that is still not all of it. You are capable of much more.

Let's take another step. Can you increase your level of mental alertness just by telling yourself 'I want to become 10% more alert'? Well can you physically increase the brightness of a light? Only by changing the light bulb for one with a higher wattage!

It's the same as trying to raise your perception or broaden your experience – you have to decide to do it and then you have to put the decision into action. That power is in your hands. You can choose how to use your own energy in interactions with other human beings.

Now do you understand why I was so fascinated by the power of Attention? Increasing my attention allowed me to control my life energies. When I turned the power of mental alertness onto another human being, it created magical moments in my life. I want you to experience the same! You can switch Attention on or off, turn it higher or lower, make it brighter or darker, focused or blurry. It is all in your own hands!

How to use your Attention to live a more satisfying and fulfilling life is the heart of this book. I will show you how to use it to create real and authentic relationships, win new business, and help more clients.

THE RAINBOW OF ATTENTION

Once I was reflecting on Attention to other people and realised that Attention comes in different varieties. In order to be able to use the right attention in the right moments with the right people, one must learn to distinguish the different types of Attention. This is particularly important for those who practice the 'Art of Attentional Networking' (a concept I am very excited about and which we will explain in a specific chapter dedicated to it in this book). Once you understand intellectually, I want you to put it immediately into action in your daily life situations.

What is the difference between these types of Attention? What I am about to tell you is very important, for everyone, but particularly for those who are interested in improving their lives and surrounding themselves with other great human beings.

I will try to explain simply, but then you will have to take action and make the connection with your own personal life. Otherwise, it remains only a theory.

Giving attention vs. getting attention

"You're coming with me," she said.
"Me? Where to?" I asked.

46

I met my dear wife 23 years ago. A beautiful Dutch lady who'd come to live in my homeland for a year and found her destiny with me. At this time, we were still dating.

"Where are we going? You look so excited... like a child."
"My boss got tickets for the opening of a special park which is going to be called 'Holland Park'." She was talking so fast that she was out of breath. "The Queen of the Netherlands will be there as a guest of honour."
"So?"
"So my boss cannot make it and proposed that I go with you since I am Dutch. It will probably be more exciting for me," she stopped and waited for my reaction. "We are going," she said.

It was a short and exciting event. Only a few VIP guests had been invited – and us. We enjoyed sharing the celebration with this small community of Dutch people in Israel. Afterwards, we walked back to our car taking a short cut down an alley.

We heard a car approaching us from behind so we moved to the side and waited for it to pass. It was the queen's car! Suddenly it felt as though we were in a slow motion movie. The car drove past and the queen looked at us with a big smile on her face. She waved goodbye to us, and it was as though she was saying 'bedankt' ('thank you' in Dutch). The car continued past and disappeared into the traffic.

My girlfriend and I looked at each other, finding it hard to believe what had just happened. Did the Queen of Holland really wave at us? Or had she been waving at someone else? We looked around; we were alone.

I meet a lot of interesting people and VIPs, and would never have thought that a wave from a queen would move me so much. But it did. It felt – and still feels – special and unique. We got precious seconds of attention that felt like eternity. We really felt the power of attention from another human being that day!

During my research, I found a lot of articles about how to get attention, how to market to yourself, how to get attention at specific occasions, or for specific opportunities and so on. But are the people who are trying to get your attention responsible for your attention? Do they decide how much attention you give? How skilled you are with it? Or is it maybe something that belongs to you, 100% belongs to you? You are in control, you decide if you want to give your attention or not. So I think GIVING ATTENTION is a far more important concept than getting attention.

Your ability to give attention to other people and to connect with them with sincerity and authenticity will decide your level of success. The ability to get attention from somebody else very much depends on you. You may decide to give your attention to only one person. That will take you far in life and bring you much more success than thinking in terms of getting attention. Companies that want your attention are actually distracting you from something more important. They try to grab your attention (I call this 'fake' or 'interest driven' attention). The media, especially social media, does everything it can to get your attention these days. Who needs more distraction!

Giving attention is much more powerful than getting attention. Giving attention comes from the heart; it's something that you want to give to someone else. Getting attention is all about taking and the attention hunters are not above using manipulation and other tricks. This is not the purpose of attention.

If attention is a psychological state of mental alertness, then only you can be in charge of it. You decide how to be alert, when to be alert and with whom you want to share your attention. You and nobody else!

There is no sophisticated research comparing giving attention with getting attention. The literature on ADHD talks about it, but only in the context of giving attention to the children to help them overcome their difficulties. Now imagine giving attention to a stranger, someone with whom you'll have no continued connection. Is that meaningful? Yes, it is.

When marketers work on getting attention, they have a specific product and target group in mind. When you give attention, it doesn't have to be targeted or have any intention behind it. You can give it to everybody all the time. It's a matter of choice. It's the ability to live your life fully and happily. When you give authentic attention, expect to be surprised, because people will want to reward you for the gift you have given them.

Positive Attention vs. Negative Attention

Most of us interact with other people every day. Make the most of them — give positive attention and enjoy those moments with other people, even strangers!

But what is positive attention? Isn't attention itself positive? I think that positive attention is the way you share delight and warmth with other people through:

- Showing real curiosity in their interests, activities and achievements.
- Smiling at other people, a real authentic smile.
- Making eye contact and using caring facial expressions (no need for words!)
- Being physically gentle and caring with other people.
- Using positive words to encourage other people.

There are plenty of opportunities to give positive attention to other people and send them the message that they are special and important, but most people choose to ignore these opportunities.

When I first began training, coaching and leading the business development of many global professional firms and SMEs, the first thing I noticed was the lack of interest in giving positive attention to other people. Be it their co-worker, a client, a supplier or a prospect. Positive attention is always the place to start. With the right positive attention to other people, the rest will fall into place.

To establish relationships built on trust and authenticity, you have to engage. To engage you need to communicate and to communicate you need to give positive attention. Consistent positive attention toward other individuals (and even collective positive attention to a company as a collection of individuals) will open a lot of doors and build real relationships. Positive attention is vital to the relationship-building process, and thankfully, it is 100% controlled by you! You have a choice about whether to give positive attention or negative attention to another human being. The more positive and authentic your attention, the more likely the other person will want to connect with you, and the more likely they will be interested in your product or service.

Is positive attention effective?

I'm frequently asked this question. Does positive attention really work? Can it get me more business? Can I really improve my relationship with my clients? My answer to all these questions is absolutely YES.

We all need to know that at least one person sees us as a capable human being who brings pleasure to others. Positive attention, reactions and responses from you let other people really feel how valued they are. Right from the beginning of your interaction with anyone, it's critical that they have experiences that show you value them. You can achieve it mostly by showing real positive attention. Later in this book, I will explain in more detail the power of 'random positive attention' and how to use it to build your relationships with others.

If you are a parent or are close to other children in your family, you know that a child develops his self-image over time. This self-image depends very much on the kind of attention the child gets from his parents and other important people in his life. The more positive attention the child receives, the healthier his self-image will be. This same self-image will determine what sort of relationships he builds with others, his self-confidence, and whether he wants to help others or not. Research has shown that people who give more positive attention to others learned this behaviour pattern from loving parents who smiled at them more and paid them plenty of attention when they were children. Do you see how important positive attention is now?

I believe that feelings of security and safety have direct links to positive attention. When I was a boy and I was frightened by the dark or a scary movie, I'd go to my mother for reassurance and support. She always helped me feel safe and secure.

You probably already know that if you want to build positive attention, you need to surround yourself with other people who have the same positive attitude. You need to avoid any distractions from people who want to steal your attention or from those who give only negative attention. If the people you spend most of your time with are positive, caring, and authentic then you become the same way too!

So what is negative attention?

Negative attention can sometimes simply be a lack of positive attention. Let's take children as an example. It's been proven that children develop signs of stress if their parents are regularly unavailable to give positive attention and take care of their immediate needs.

When these children grow up they will probably lack empathy for others. They find it difficult to give empathy because they cast the other person in the role of the one who failed them when they were children. Since they do not believe that the other person can give them anything, they fail to pay them positive attention (negative attention). And so the cycle continues.

In some cases people actively give negative attention to others. It may be in the way they look at someone, or how they treat them or talk to them. Actively ignoring or ostracizing someone is a favourite trick of the negative attention giver. I'm sure you've experienced some of these 'gifts'. I have many times, right from elementary school to the present day. But I've learned how to deal with it. You can refuse to accept negative attention, that way it has no power to hurt you.

I want to repeat this last point again as it's very important to me that you understand it. Every act of attention takes two parties – the giver and the receiver. The receiver can choose to refuse the attention; they are not obliged to take it. We will deal with this secret of attention later on, but please hold it in mind until then.

While you read these lines ask yourself this question: are you a negative attention giver? Are you a person who goes around with a sour face, who complains all the time, who looks at others with anger or coldness? If so, this means that you are habituated to a world of negative attention. I suggest that you take a look at how you got there and why you choose to stay.

Some people thrive on negative attention. In most cases, it's probably the only attention they know. If they have only ever received negative attention, then they think that is all there is. They don't even know its 'negative' – to them it's just attention.

Second, negative attention seems more 'fun'. It is dynamic and dramatic and people, by nature, are more interested in dramatic interactions (even if they are negative).

Third, a person's mood can influence the type of attention he gives. Unfortunately many people are constantly in a bad mood, and so they treat other people the way they feel.

Lastly, giving negative attention seems much easier to give than positive attention. I disagree with that, but unfortunately I seem to be in the minority.

If you feel that it would be hard for you to feel or act with positive attention on a daily basis, it may be worth seeking professional help and advice. You are very welcome to contact me as well. It will be fun showing you how we can turn negative attention into positive attention and seeing the immediate impact this will have on your life and level of success!

Active Attention vs. Passive Attention

Two other major forms of attention are: passive Attention and active Attention. Passive attention is caused by an involuntary reaction to external events, such as a bright flash, a strong odour, or a sudden loud noise. We might say that because passive attention is involuntary, it is easy. It's a reaction rather than a response. Active attention is voluntary and is guided by alertness, concentration, interest and needs such as curiosity and hunger. Active attention takes effort (Gaddes, 1994).
In other words, in the passive state our attention is captured by what's in front of us. Our thoughts and feelings involuntarily react to the spectacle, without requiring any active attention from us.

Remember the last time you attended an event and while listening to a presentation, your thoughts, boredom, or daydreams took your attention away from the speaker? You heard without listening and saw without noticing. This is passive attention.

Another example is when you enter a room in your home and can't remember why. You know that a mere moment before you had a reason for going to that room, but now that you are there, you cannot recall it. Passive attention brought you here. Passive attention is why you sometimes call the wrong number, because it's a habit to call this number all the time.
Sometimes passive attention can give you energy. But when you overindulge in it, passive attention can be enervating.

Active attention, on the other hand, is a multidimensional cognitive process that includes the ability to select and focus on what is important at any given moment. It is a complex process that includes feeling alert and aroused, selecting what we should be attending to, ignoring what we don't want to attend to, and maintaining our focus for the right amount of time. Attention allows us to plan or preview and monitor and regulate our thoughts and actions also with regards to our interaction with other people.

Spontaneous Attention vs. Planned Attention

Recently, I had an interesting discussion with two friends about an event we were all supposed to attend. I was to be the keynote speaker. Those of you who have participated in any of my events know that I do not like boring presentations and I always like to surprise attendees. (If you haven't been to one of my events, please come and join me. It will make my day if you mention this part of the book). One of my friends suggested I plan ahead while the other thought I should be more spontaneous.

Are you a planner or do you thrive on spontaneity? If you're going out on a date, do you plan it in advance? Your answer will tell you if you're someone who wings it or someone who prefers to plan ahead.

When it is about giving attention to other people, I enjoy being spontaneous. I sincerely believe that spontaneous attention is real attention; it is the way to express authentic attention toward another human being.

A compliment is one way of giving authentic positive attention to another person. How would you feel if a stranger approached you on the street and gave you a compliment about your tie or your shoes?

I know... I know what you are thinking. Unfortunately, many strangers who approach us on the street want to sell us something, or want money or just to ask for directions. (I'm ignoring more annoying situations such as sexual harassment). Everybody learns to deal with these situations in their own way. Some are happy to help, while others prefer to pass by.

Let's go back to the situation I described. Imagine you're in a shopping mall and suddenly a passerby gives you a compliment: 'Nice shoes!' That's real spontaneous Attention. What do you feel? Isn't it a kind of strange warm feeling inside? 'Somebody noticed me, they liked something about me. A stranger gave me a compliment, somebody I do not know and will never see again, somebody who had no interest in selling me something. Isn't it wonderful?' Now imagine, that minutes before encountering this other human being, you'd felt a bit sad or maybe half asleep. Will this sincere spontaneous attention wake you up? Give you a positive boost (even for a few seconds of your life)? I want you to close your eyes and experience this situation deep inside your heart. I love these magical moments!

You're probably wondering why Planned Attention is needed if Spontaneous Attention is so great. In some situations it's better to be prepared about the attention you are about to give to others. Moreover, you need to plan who you will share this planned attention with. I work with Planned Attention whenever I participate in a large event. I like to look at the list of participants and see who is attending. If I know any of them, I can prepare to give them attention at a specific time.

But guess what? While writing this I've thought of another possibility. How about using Planned Spontaneous Attention? You could decide that every day you will give three people some real sincere attention. You do not know who they are – it could be your spouse, your children, your boss, your colleague, a client or even a stranger. You do not know when you will give the attention, or what the attention will be, but you know for sure that you will give it. You can do it personally, face-to-face (always much more powerful) or over the phone.

Why not try it? This would be especially helpful if you are a planner. Don't worry about the results, just do it! I'm sure you will be positively surprised. I know that it will have a direct positive influence on your life. You will cherish these moments (and others as well). I would be delighted to get an email from you describing these moments and your feelings... Go. Try. Share.

Of course you can use a mix of all the above attention varieties. You can give Passive Spontaneous Positive Attention or even Active Negative Planned Attention (I don't recommend the latter!) The choice is completely yours. Make use of the rainbow of attention to shine right through someone else's fog of gloom and doom. In later chapters, you'll learn more authentic Attention techniques and tips, not only to build your success but to support other people – the two go together, remember?

Trust me, they will both surprise you and give you plenty of ideas and practical solutions that you can start using in your work and personal life straightaway... Just keep reading.

PAY ATTENTION: YOUNG VS. OLD

Does age play a role in someone's ability to give attention to others? Surely emotional maturity is a vital factor in building positive, long-lasting relationships, so it stands to reason that older people are better at paying attention. But is that really the case?

Experiments conducted in 1982 by Prof. Benjamin Somberg and Dr. Timothy A. Salthouse, checked divided attention and adult aging, taking into account age differences in single-task performance and measuring divided attention independently of resource allocation strategies. All the experiments showed that age difference didn't play much of a role in the divided attention ability of each group.

History teaches us, time after time, that it is always (or at least most of the time) wise to pay attention to people who are older and more experienced. Moreover, isn't your grey hair, if you have any, perceived as being smarter, more skillful and with greater ability to understand others? My business travels take me many times to India. I do remember some years ago, while travelling to India, I met with one of the most interesting guys in my life. I cannot explain in words the power of his look, but there was some rare beauty in his eyes. It was like a magnet that attracted me, without my control, to look directly into his eyes. The people around him considered him the holy guru. Thousands of people were standing in line, every day, to meet with this guru, each in his turn, that did not last more than 30 seconds. Now, with reflection to that moment, I am totally convinced that his old age, the authority and his wisdom, made his attention giving act a very powerful one, one that moved your heart. No words needed.

But is that applicable also in our days, that older people give much 'better' attention than young ones? In many cases, nowadays, the young person, our kids for example, has much more knowledge than their parents, the older generation?

What if we are dealing with giving attention to the other person? Do you really think that we tend to give easier attention to older people? Or maybe more the opposite? How much influence does the age of the person giving the attention have? Is there a difference between the attention given by a young person to an old person and the attention given by a young person to other young person? And what about attention given by an old person to a young person; is that more powerful and influential? Does the relationship between the old and young have any importance, e.g. in case the old person who is giving the attention is a parent, boss or teacher of the young person.

I think that sometimes an attention given by a child of five can be much more pure and authentic. For a start, this attention won't be based on self-interest or ego. But isn't having understanding of the attention an important part of the act itself? A young kid does not understand that what she is doing, so can it really be defined as 'giving attention'? As my focus is on the result rather than the intention, I don't think that understanding attention is vital to giving attention. If you disagree we have something to discuss at our next meeting!

On the other hand, if an older person gives an attention – either positive or negative – to a younger person, it will surely be taken seriously by the latter. When we were kids, my four sisters and I would often visit other family members with my parents. If one of us misbehaved, my mother did not have to yell at us. She only had to open her big brown eyes wide and we'd immediately know to change our behaviour. Her positive attentions, compliments and encouragement were just as effective.

Let me summarize by saying that the age has some effects in the act of giving attention. But I still have my doubts if the attention given by an older person has more effect than attention given by a young person. One thing is certain, just as your character, emotions, and convictions are not subject to decay, neither is your attention. And giving attention helps us to stay young at heart.

PAY ATTENTION: WOMEN VS. MEN

Who do you think tend to be a better attention giver – women or men? Who have a shorter attention span? Or maybe you are more interested to know why this is a matter at all? I will try to answer these questions.

Research shows that there are differences between the male and female brain and it has been scientifically proven that men and women are biologically wired to pay attention to different things. Male and female brains mature at different speeds. Gender and hormones influence how the human brain develops. For example, women have to deal with attention problems more frequently (especially during their reproductive years) because of hormone fluctuations. Since attention hinges on mental alertness, we can see why men and women often have different learning styles and behavioural patterns. These differences are based in physiology.

Anthropologists Daniel Maltz and Ruth Borker from Stanford University came to the conclusion that there are differences in how men and women show attention (at least in the US, where their research was conducted). Women often used minimal responses, like 'hmm' or 'oh', to show their attention and encourage the other person to continue speaking and sharing. Conversely, men used and interpreted these minimal responses as a kind of agreement or approval. This difference could explain men's tendency to use minimal responses less frequently than women, as well as women's belief that men do not pay attention to them when they speak.

What about same-gender and cross-gender attention? Do you think there is a difference in the level and quality of attention given? Or doesn't the gender of the attention-giver and receiver have a bearing on the interaction?

Gender definitely has an effect. For example, it seems that men are men's best friends. Men understand men. Men generally respect one another until one proves himself unworthy of that respect. It is easier for a man to give attention to another man for all sorts of reasons, including cultural ones. If a man concentrates too much attention on another woman (not his significant other or any other family member), people may get the wrong interpretation.

AUTHENTIC ATTENTION™: VALUING YOURSELF AND OTHERS

"You can make more friends
in two months by becoming
genuinely interested in other people
than you can in two years
by trying to get
others interested in you."

Dale Carnegie

Let me repeat that: "You can make more friends in two months by becoming genuinely interested in other people than you can in two years by trying to get others interested in you".

Dale Carnegie continued: "Yet I know and you know people who blunder through life trying to badger other people into becoming interested in them. Of course, it doesn't work. People are not interested in you.

They are not interested in me. They are interested in themselves – morning, noon, and after dinner."

Do you genuinely care about other people? Do you give others authentic attention™?

When I was acting managing director for an international tax and financial consultancy, I introduced weekly one-on-one meetings with every person on my team. Plus I'd regularly walk around and talk to our employees. These were my ways of showing our people that I was interested in them and their work; I was aware of their existence and thankful that they served our company. I made a point of being available. This alone helped us keep our employees longer and they worked harder too. People respond to people who are sincerely interested in them.

Authentic attention™ is a basic need in human psychology. Didn't you feel good the last time somebody gave you authentic attention™? Other people's attention makes us feel special and significant. We want to be around those who give us attention. And we tend to reciprocate their interest by showing interest in them.

There are simple ways to show authentic attention™, like speaking in a sympathetic tone during phone calls. I believe you can hear someone smile when they're talking on the phone, you do not need to see them. It's the same when you encounter somebody you know by chance and they express genuine pleasure. People, whoever they are, respond immediately to an authentic expression of warmth. So be sincere. Authentic heartfelt interest builds over time.

Such displays of attention giving are the foundations of successful business and human relationships. They are small reminders that say: "I noticed you. You are significant to me. I care." Who wouldn't want such authentic attention?

I lost my beloved mother this year. It was a sad and sudden death and left all of us with broken hearts. Hundreds, if not thousands, of people went to the funeral. It was amazing to learn how many people loved my mom. How many people she'd helped, supported and touched during her life. The phone didn't stop ringing at our house. What was nearly as shocking as my mother's death was the fact that she probably didn't know how many people loved her. Do you want to know what makes me really sad? Only a few of these people had ever told her how they felt.

Allow me to give you some advice my dear reader – don't make the same mistake. When you care about someone and want to give her your authentic attention, let that person know. Do it while you have the chance.

I remember arriving late one night at the Taj West End hotel in Bangalore, India. I was the keynote speaker in a conference the next day. I was tired and hungry and I really wanted some Mediterranean food. The night chef, who'd worked at one of the best hotels in the UAE, must have heard me. Within 20 minutes I was served a light Mediterranean dinner. I cannot tell you how happy this made me! Who wouldn't appreciate this kind of attention?

Is it hard? Do you need special skills? Thankfully, authentic attention is easy to learn and very gratifying. All it takes is awareness, a realization of how important it is and a little bit of practice. Before you know it, you'll be expressing attention and sincerely giving authentic attention to people around you. The ability to give authentic attention will help you grow beyond your comfort zone and ensure you spend less time dwelling on your own problems.

The more you give sincere and authentic attention to others, the more rewarding your personal and business relationships will be. Worth it, right? It'll be fun too. It will help you develop new relationships, boost your self-confidence and give you the opportunity to discover different worlds and cultures.

Dale Carnegie understood this. He wrote:

> "If you want others to like you.
> If you want to develop real friendship,
> if you want to help others at the same time
> as you help yourself, keep this principle in mind:
> become genuinely interested in other people."

Or, as I would put it, become an Authentic Attention expert.

"Give whatever
you are doing
and whoever
you are with
the gift of
your attention."

Jim Rohn

CHAPTER 2

PAYING ATTENTION

FIVE SECRETS
REVEALED

"The simple act
of paying
positive attention
to people
has a great deal
to do with
productivity."

Tom Peters

CHAPTER 2: PAYING ATTENTION - FIVE SECRETS REVEALED

FIVE BEST-KEPT SECRETS

I want to share with you the five best-kept secrets about Attention. These secrets govern every creative and productive process in your life: from childhood to adulthood, and from your personal life to your career. All of these secrets operate through constant and dynamic exchange. Understanding these secrets will help you practice the Law of Paying Attention. If you want attention and appreciation, you need to give attention and appreciation.

SECRET #1: GIVING! GIVING! GIVING!

The power of giving

When I told my close friends that I was writing a book about attention that stressed giving attention rather that getting it, each of them reminded me that giving attention always leads to getting attention. Funnily enough you often get much more attention than you originally gave.

You'll already have gathered that I travel a great deal and spend a lot of time in hotels and restaurants because of my consulting and public speaking business. One of my favourite pastimes when I'm on the road is people-watching.

I can always spot the guests who give attention to the hotel's staff. Everywhere in the world, it is the same. Whoever they are, the cleaning lady who cleans your room and gets you clean towels and a fresh bowl of fruits, or the doorman, the bellboy, the waiter at the restaurant etc. They always stand out – it's like magic. How do I know? I don't have to eavesdrop to know when people are really connecting. I can see it in the interest on the guest's face as they listen to the hotel employee's stories and recommendations. We all want to be listened to, right? And what happens next? The hotel employees always find a way to give back to the guest. They need to give back immediately, not because they were told to or because they'll get a generous tip, but just because they feel like it.

If you don't believe me try it yourself on your next visit to a restaurant or hotel. You will be amazed at the results! You will be amazingly surprised for good!

This is one of the basic secrets of Attention. The more you give it, sincerely, the more you get it back. Giving attention to others makes things happen, not only in the hospitality industry but in every area of life. The basic idea behind giving attention is to consciously help and participate in the universal flow of abundance. You can achieve it by simply following these actions:

i.   Don't wait – give attention daily

You have countless opportunities every day to give your attention to other people. You can do it by giving somebody a genuine smile or compliment. Focus on leaving the other person feeling great, better than she felt before interacting with you.

ii.   Don't keep score – give freely

When you look at life, it's clear that when you fully give something valuable it always multiplies. Intention is everything. So make it your intention to give without keeping score. Forget about self-interest, just give from your heart—this sort of attention can be truly powerful and life-changing.

iii.   Don't be afraid to get – give and have the grace to receive

It's a common trait of habitual givers: they do not know how to receive. I used to be one of these givers until I learned better. Imagine giving an attention to someone you love who refuses to accept it. Would you be disappointed? Sad? Maybe you'd even start doubting yourself? Now let's say the other person happily receives your gift; how would you feel now? Good, right? So be open to receiving attention from others. Thus, others will accept your attention when you sincerely give it to them.

iv.   Don't ignore yourself – give from yourself

Giving attention presupposes that we have something to give, something that comes from the heart with all the best intentions. Attention comes from our being, from who we are; for we can only give what we have. Like a car, you can't run on empty and you certainly can't give from empty. So take care of yourself – give yourself more joyful moments, a healthy routine, and look after your body. That way you will be able to give more to others. Remember: to give attention is to give a part of yourself to others, so make sure it is healthy and happy!

v.   Don't dream – give and be present

To give attention is to give an intangible gift to another person. So when you give attention you must be fully present, listening carefully and actively. Stop multitasking! Concentrate only on the person in front of you. Challenging? Maybe. But the rewards are enormous. Give your full open-hearted presence and the universe will take care of the rest.

Empower your giving possibilities

Giving attention to others will improve all of your giving abilities and make you more effective and efficient in your daily activities. Your ability to give others attention, to let the energy of others shine, enables you to leverage yourself so that you accomplish far more in far less time than the average person.

During 20 years of working in the corporate sector, I discovered that the more I empowered, inspired and motivated others around me, the more they wanted to be part of my team and support me in achieving my goals. They knew if I did well I'd make sure they did too. Giving attention to others will activate new positive energies and enthusiasm in them. It will boost their self-esteem. You help them feel remember that they are valuable, significant, worthwhile.

Attention giving means really listening – concentrating and being sincerely interested in what someone is sharing with you. Listen to others every day: you'll empower them and help them feel good about themselves. The more you do it, the more you'll want to do it and you'll get better the more that you practice too.

Many have written about the psychological law of reciprocity. In 'Motivating Others Toward Peak Performance', Brian Tracy says, "If you make me feel good about myself, I will find a way to make you feel good about yourself." People will always look for ways to reciprocate your kindnesses toward them.

So what's stopping you from saying and doing things that make other people feel good? I promise you that if you make it a daily habit, you'll be astonished at how good it makes you feel and at the wonderful things that will begin to happen all around you.

The power to cope with challenges

Challenges are part of life. There will always be obstacles between you and your goals. So how do cope with them?

Attention, like intelligence and money, helps you triumph over life challenges. Let me explain.

Take for example ADHD (attention deficit hyperactivity disorder). The primary recommendation for parents is to invest more attention in the child who suffers with ADHD; this helps improve their child's social skills.

A similar solution can be given in case of people suffering from economical problems or any other sort of socioeconomic disadvantages. What if you cannot afford to attend college, but want to compete in the workplace with people who have a degree? Your ability to give attention to other people will definitely help you out in the workplace. Education is a fine thing, but never underestimate the power of likeability.

If you are a parent, your ability to give authentic attention to your children will have a tremendous impact on their future success. I've always believed that my successful social relationships are a direct result of positive parenting and growing up in a supportive family.

Giving authentic attention will get you and others through life challenges, no matter how complex they may be.

Have you ever almost missed your flight? It's happened to me several times, but there's one time I will always remember. I'd spoken at an event in Tokyo and was due to catch an early flight, so I programmed the alarms on my phone and on the hotel TV. I slept through both of them and woke 1.5 hours before my flight's scheduled departure. I was frantic because if I didn't get this flight I'd be late for another appointment in New York. I sprinted downstairs to the lobby to see if there was anything I could do.

I'd helped the hotel's concierge while I'd been staying there, giving him a lot of my personal attention (he'd been having a difficult time with his daughter), so he did everything in his power to help me. Within 15 minutes I was on board a helicopter flying to Tokyo international airport – it had been arranged especially for me. There was a limo waiting to drive me directly to my plane. Guess what – this VIP treatment cost nothing! Although you could say I'd already paid with my authentic attention and willingness, to help another person won me again a life challenge and sweet memory.

Help others shine

I am writing this just after arriving home from an amazing conference in Philadelphia, where I gave a keynote presentation on the "Art of Attentional Networking" (I dedicated a separate chapter in my book for this interesting subject).

There was a two hour wait before my flight back home, so my colleague and I went to a gadget store at the airport. I didn't plan to buy anything. As usual, I was soon in conversation with the saleslady. She was tired after a long shift, and I, as you've probably figured out, love interacting with others (especially strangers, it gives the conversation a real purity). We were laughing and enjoying the discussion. After a few minutes John, the manager of the store, (I promised you, John, I would dedicate these lines to you!) joined the conversation. It was so joyful. It was the sort of conversation where you feel like you are buddies and have known each other for at least 20 years.

Both my colleague and I ended up buying a shoulder massage instrument. When we got home my colleague's machine worked but mine didn't. I searched the Internet and found the company's website. To get my machine checked I needed to fill in two forms and send the machine, with the forms and a copy of the receipt, to the company headquarters in LA. It would take up to 60 days for my machine to be checked. Frustrating! I wanted my machine now! I hadn't even used it yet! Not to mention the cost of sending it from Europe to the US for a machine that only cost $19.99!

But then I had another idea. I had the original receipt with the telephone number of the store I'd bought it from. John, the store manager, picked up and recognized my voice immediately: "Itzik, is that you? What took you so long?" My heart filled with warmth. John remembered me. From all the hundreds of people who passed through his store in Philly airport he remembered me! I explained the situation and he immediately told me not to bother. "Just send in the original machine and email us your home address, the cost of sending it to the USA and your bank account details. I'll send you a new one right away and we'll refund the shipping costs direct to your account. Lovely to meet you Itzik, I want you to know that you changed my life."

I am not trying to impress you but to impress upon you, my friend, how giving sincere attention to others makes them shine! I have no doubt that another customer would probably have had to go through the usual procedure to get their machine fixed. But in this case, John created his own procedure just because he felt like doing so. He wasn't obliged to. And it could be that we will never meet again. The fact is some people receive better service than others. Why? If you give attention you will inspire others to give back.

It's been shown over and over again in ADHD studies that parents who give authentic and dedicated attention to their child get much better results. Studies by hospitals also show that children with ADHD who regularly receive attention from their parents and other people who are close to them are more likely to get better and to stop their medication.

Last year, my beloved mother passed away. Just after she took her last breath, my father stood up and asked the doctor and the nurses to join us. He wanted to thank them. My father gave a short speech right there during the saddest moment of his life. He gave real authentic attention to the strangers who'd taken care of my mother in her last moments. Why did he do it? My mother had already passed away so it would not help her. No, he wasn't thinking about what he needed. He was thinking about them: he wanted to give these people, who do such holy work, his pure attention. He made a dark moment SHINE. He helped them to shine and I'm sure that my mother was shining with them. I am proud of you Dad!

I hope you understand that this first secret of Attention – the ability to give without limit, with authenticity – gets real results. Wherever you are and whatever you do, you can make other people shine, when you 'hug' them with your attention.

SECRET #2: The meeting point between non-verbal communication and the subconscious mind

"When you do the common things in life
in an uncommon way,
you will command the attention
of the world."

George Washington Carver

Soaring self-esteem

Will you believe me if I share with you that people who give attention to others have more energy and enjoy a better and healthier quality of life? One of the main reasons is because giving attention makes your self-esteem soar.

We've already explored how giving sincere and authentic attention to others attracts reciprocal attention from them. This reciprocated interest boosts your self-esteem. And medical research has proven that strong self-esteem can overcome physical injury and symptoms caused by or associated with stress.

When you pay attention to others you are far more likely to make friends and create stronger social contacts. Your positive energy, attitude and interest in others attracts people to you so new friendships come easily. On the other hand, if you tend to have a negative attitude, don't show sincere interest in other people or give them your attention, you will most probably have fewer close relationships in your life. Chances are you'll be lonely.

Loneliness has a direct impact on your physical well-being. It can affect your immune system and even damage your subconscious mind.

Extensive research by medical schools around the world and in Europe in particular, shows that the 'attention' factor has a real effect on health.

Consider the last time you were going through tough times. Who helped you? I assume it was your family and friends, the same people who give you attention regularly. This social support system is a result of your ability to give attention to them. You built it with your own hands. The more attention you give to other people, the more friends you will have. The more friends you have, the stronger your support system will be.

So next time one of your friends is suffering or hospitalized, make the effort and visit them. This is an opportunity to give real attention and relieve some of their pain. Not to mention the fact that it will make your friendship even stronger.

I know many couples who have a wonderful relationship. When I ask them the secret of their closeness they always say that sincere focused attention during painful times bonded them forever. It created a powerful connection that nobody can take away from them.

I saw this in action during a recent documentary about a Brazilian couple. All her life, the woman had suffered from a rare genetic illness and was mostly bedbound. She had to use a wheelchair to get around. On the other hand, her husband was an extreme sportsman who'd won many medals. Why would a man like that choose to marry a woman who needed constant medical treatment and who spent so much time in hospital? I think I know the answer.

The ability to give attention to another human being bonds you so closely that you almost cannot see physical disability. The physical becomes irrelevant – it is the love and attention that counts. Giving attention is such a powerful tool that it dominates your subconscious mind with positivity.

Be welcome anywhere

Whenever somebody has a photo taken with me I always point my finger at them. Do you want to know why? Let me answer that by asking you a question: when you're in a group photo, whose picture do you look for first?

I don't take photos merely to impress others. Nor do I take them so I'll become famous and get more attention. I take photos so that I can help other people shine. By pointing my index finger toward the other person(s) in the photo, I direct attention to them. It's another way for me to give attention to other people.

It doesn't matter what you do for a living: you have to be interested in other people if you want to be successful. If that is true of photos, you can be sure it is true when dealing with people face-to-face.

Can you guess which two factors played a crucial part in my success and that of other people? No, it isn't knowledge. In my case, it was not my cross-border legal knowledge that made me a respected international lawyer and gave me the opportunity to work with famous clients. I believe that extremely successful people do two things that other people don't do. First, they understand and master human nature.

Everything they do, every movement, every gesture, the way they use their voice, has been carefully rehearsed in advance so that their subconscious mind channels it automatically. Second, they give authentic attention to other people.

You can do the same. Every time you encounter another human being in a meeting or conference, say this silently to yourself: "Thank you for coming into my life. I am grateful to meet and listen to you. I am going to give you the very best attention I possibly can." It doesn't just work one-to-one, it works with audiences too. These words are a command to both your subconscious mind and your body, and both will respond accordingly and get you the results you want.

During my corporate career, I discovered you can win the attention, time and cooperation of even the most famous people by becoming genuinely interested in them. Let me give you an example.

How many times have you been to lunch or had a meeting with a famous author or actress? Every time I read an interesting book, I look up the author's email address and send her a letter or postcard. I tell them that I admire their work and would love to meet to learn the secrets of their success. Sounds like a silly idea? Guess what, the fact that 99% of us don't do that makes you unique. You showed a real interest and you gave real attention to another human being. This is always appreciated, and many times I've been rewarded by being invited to meet the celebrity.

If you want to make friends or attract new clients, if you want to be remembered, then put yourself out to do things that show real attention to other people – things that require energy and time, unselfish acts that are unmotivated by self-interest.

Open up your communication skills

Some time ago, at a professional conference in Kiev, Ukraine, I noticed a lady standing by herself at the side of the room.

Now for many years, I was not a talker. I would stand at the side of the room, too shy to talk to anyone. Or at least, I thought I was shy. Then in 2005 I went on a life-changing training course. The course taught me that I wasn't shy, at all, just very closed. In elementary school I'd enjoyed a very happy social life and had many friends. Instinct – and my family's excellent example – had taught me how to give everybody my sincere attention. Then one day, five guys beat me up. That incident closed me down for more than two decades. So I was not shy, I was closed. And now I am opening up again and being myself.

Why have I told you this story? Because this woman in Ukraine reminded me of whom I'd used to be. I'm always especially interested in giving my sincere attention to people like that.

So I approached her. In the beginning she was a bit unsure of herself. After a while I told her about a recent visit to Colombia and she shared with me that she was a CFO for one of the largest energy concerns in the Russian CIS (Commonwealth of Independent States). She talked for almost 30 minutes. She was not interested in my stories, all what she wanted was to be listened to by an authentic listener. She almost seemed afraid that if she stopped talking I'd leave her and she did not want that to happen.

As I said, I was in a conference with hundreds of other participants, and by choosing to talk to one lady I actually ignored everybody else! At the end she thanked me for our interesting conversation and three months later she became a client.

You're probably thinking 'what conversation? You hardly said anything!' That's true, but I still gave her authentic attention by listening so intently. I was genuinely interested in her story. And she felt it. Authentic rapt attention, true listening, is one of the best gifts you can give.
Paying exclusive authentic attention to a person who is talking to you is a very important element in improving your communication skills. If you want to show somebody that you really care, stop whatever you are doing when they talk to you and listen. Unfortunately, listening is not the norm. In too many conversations, people are so concerned with what they were going to say next that they don't keep their ears open. It seems that the ability to give attention is rarer than almost any other trait.

Have you ever spoken to a friend and afterwards felt as though a weight had been lifted from you? That's what attention feels like. Sometimes you don't want advice, just a friendly, attentive listener to whom you can open your heart. This isn't only true in personal relationships – I think clients sometimes want that too.

Giving concentrated attention definitely boosts your communication skills. In 'How to Win Friends and Influence People', Dale Carnegie quotes a man who'd met Sigmund Freud, one of the greatest listeners of modern times: "It struck me so forcibly that I shall never forget him.

He had qualities which I had never seen in any other man. Never had I seen such concentrated attention. There was none of that piercing 'soul penetrating gaze' business. His eyes were mild and genial. His voice was low and kind. His gestures were few. But the attention he gave me, his appreciation of what I said, even when I said it badly, was extraordinary. You've no idea what it meant to be listened to like that."

So the next time you have a conversation act as if you're Sigmund Freud. Be a good conversationalist, be an active and attentive listener. If you want to be interesting, be interested. Ask questions that put the other person at ease and they will enjoy answering them. Encourage them to talk about themselves and their achievements. Everyone's much more interested in their own troubles and desires than they are in someone else's. I am sure if you follow my simple advice you will create magic in the other person's life and open up new possibilities for yourself.

Convince others to do what you want

Do you want to learn how to make people happy to go along with your suggestions?

When I was a trainee in a law office, I learned an important lesson about communicating with attention. I was working with the senior partner of the firm, a man with a worldwide reputation because of his expertise in international tax. He was often invited to speak at conferences, social events and professional gatherings, but because of his workload, he could not attend all of them. Sometimes he used to send one of us to represent him. (It was a great fun and a brilliant opportunity to practice my networking skills).

No-one ever felt insulted by his refusal. What was his secret? One thing's certain – he never said he had too much work to do before slamming down the phone! He always thanked them and showed appreciation for the invitation, then he would express sincere regret that he could not participate. He'd go on to suggest another respected person who could join the event instead. This helped solve the host's problem, so why would they feel unhappy about his refusal? By giving them another option, they were happy to go along with what he wanted. He understood their needs and wants and tried to accommodate them. He gave sincere attention to the other person.

To be an effective attention giver, or even an attention leader, bear the following points in mind:

i.   Be authentic – concentrate on the benefits to the other person and do not promise more than you are able to deliver.
ii.   Be empathetic – care about the other person, their needs and desires.
iii.   Be concise – know exactly what you want the other person to do, why you want them to do it and how you want them to do it.
iv.   Be caring – consider the benefits to the other person and the advantages for them in following your advice.
v.   Be kind and sincere – show the other person how they will benefit from following your request.

Will this approach always work? No, but it definitely works most of the time. This is a great way to change people's attitudes. People are more likely to do what you want them to do if you give sincere attention to them and their needs. They'll be happy to follow your suggestions.

Attention is like a muscle

Scholars and authors, including Daniel Goleman in his new book 'Focus', compare Attention to a muscle. There are mental exercises that can improve attention, that strengthen the brain, like going to the gym to strengthen your body's muscles. These exercises are simple but effective. One of the most helpful ones is called 'the Stoplight'. Goleman describes it like this: "Imagine a poster on your wall that says when you are upset, remember the stoplight. Red light: stop, calm down, and think before you act. Yellow light: think about a range of things you can do now. And what the outcome will be – green light – pick the best one and try it now." This is a highly effective way to use your subconscious mind to sharpen your attention.

SECRET #3: AN UNLIMITED BUT SELECTIVE RESOURCE

"To pay attention, this is our endless and proper work."

Mary Oliver

Your attentional filtering system

Are people always aware of what they are attending to? I would like to think that the answer is yes. Every person has the choice to deploy their attention whenever they want, to whomever they want and wherever they are. We have complete, conscious control over it. You are the only person who decides how much attention you want to give to another human being. On the other hand, life is full of surprises, and sometimes you cannot fully decide on the attention you want to give to another person. In that case surely it'd be useful to 'expect the unexpected.' But is that assumption true?

Attention is a complex phenomenon that has been extensively studied for many years. The scholars Reason & Mycielska (1982) decided that Attention is a limited resource. They believe that people have a fixed amount of attention that must be allocated according to need. If they spend it wrongly, too bad, it's gone. They compared attention to a bucket of water: every time people draw upon it there is less. With my sincere respect to the scholars, I tend to disagree with them.

Let's look at that bucket of water. Once it's empty, it can be filled with water again. And attention isn't really like water; there are lots of ways that it can be used. If you have a navigation system in your car, you probably know that it is hard to monitor the road while looking at it, but it is much easier while talking to it on a mobile phone (via a Bluetooth device!) True, you can only give full attention to one person at a time and giving attention to one person means you're not giving it to another person. Plus a person's attentional capacity varies according to circumstance.

... Sorry, I lost my concentration for a few minutes, the telephone rang and I answered it...

Since my attention was on the phone call rather than on my writing does that mean my attention is limited? Just because many things go unnoticed does that mean attention is a limited resource? I think the opposite.

When we give attention to another person, I believe we only have enough attention for them. Each of us has our own attentional filtering system that helps us concentrate on giving attention to one person while filtering out other people at the same time. This is mostly a good thing. But sometimes, due to too much information or too many people to handle, these attention filters can make a mistake and you find yourself giving your attention to the wrong person.
So while attention works best when we limit it to one person or task at a time, it is really an unlimited resource.

We just need to channel it to the right people or opportunities. Our brain can only consume and give a limited amount of attention. People attend to some things to the exclusion of others. We don't have the mental resources to attend to everything. The classic auditory example is the 'Cocktail Party Phenomenon' where you are having a conversation with one person and are generally oblivious to everything else around you, unless you consciously shift your attention. We humans have only a single stream of conscious attention, which is difficult – possibly impossible – to divide.

But one thing is very clear – who decides who you give attention to? Only YOU! Attention is unlimited in the sense that you can give as much attention as you want to however many people you want, whenever you want and wherever you are. Attention as a resource is not limited by place, time, or object constraints. This book will teach how to refill your attention 'bucket' on a daily basis. Follow its advice and you will tap into an unlimited resource. Learn to use it wisely and you will create amazing opportunities for yourself!

Enrich your knowledge

Attention is a resource. If you want to be an attention expert you need to dedicate time and energy to it. Some social experts argue that attention has become a more limited resource because we live in an age of information overload. People have become accustomed to getting information in an instant, and they will only spend time and attention on the pieces of information that interest them. As a result, people find it more challenging to focus for longer periods of time.

I take an opposing view. Indeed, the human mind is only capable of taking in a limited amount of information. Everyone has different limits. But that does not limit the attention resource. Every human being is capable of giving unlimited attention to a single source of information.

Some people seem to have short or limited attention while interacting with others, while other people easily focus and give their full attention. During my years of networking around the world, I found a pattern that could explain these differing attention spans. It seems that the relationship between the attention-giver and the attention-receiver determines the length of their attention span.

We often get so entrenched in our daily routines that we forget to learn from every interaction we have with other people. Giving people focused attention is a great way to grow, enrich your knowledge and enjoy life. These sincere interactions provide new experiences and insights while offering endless opportunities for daily learning. But learning is best when it's gained through focused attention on another person.

So how can you use your attention as an unlimited resource for learning and gaining new knowledge?

i.   **Give Attention like a child**. Ask a lot of questions. Asking questions is the number one way to learn more every day. Take me as an example; every time I need help on a specific subject, I see it as a great opportunity to interact with one of my contacts. I'll try to find one who is more knowledgeable on the subject than me and give them my full attention. Trust me, it's much more fun than searching the Internet for hours and it gets you better results. Not to mention the opportunity to strengthen your relationship with the other person.

ii.   **A damn good listening**. Listen. I mean really listen to the other person. Attention with active listening is a powerful tool that promotes learning. Years ago, when I started my public speaking career, I was advised by one of the greatest speakers of our times, the late Zig Ziglar, that great public speakers are great because they pay attention, listen to the feedback they get from the audience and respond to it accordingly. Do you do that? I think if somebody criticizes you then it's best to shut up and listen. If you look carefully you will notice that the people who criticize us are mainly those who care about us. So if you know that their intentions are good, just pay attention and listen. You will learn a lot. Attention giving by active listening will not only slow you down, it will teach you something new about things we often take for granted.

Giving attention to another person enables both of you to share valuable information and knowledge. Whether you're talking to your spouse about a serious matter, or you're in the middle of thrashing out an important business deal, then a limited or short attention span won't do you any favours. If you want to enrich your knowledge, or share significant knowledge with others, you need to be able to give unlimited attention for as long as it takes.

Research has found that shorter attention spans may be detrimental to educational achievement. Others also think that limited attention spans may interfere with productivity at work. It follows then that if you find it hard to pay attention for longer periods, you may find it difficult to build and sustain strong, deep relationships. With stakes as high as these, it is well worth making the effort to increase your attention span.

SECRET #4: IT'S UP TO YOU!

"The thought manifests as the word.
The word manifests as the deed.
The deed develops into habit.
And the habit hardens into character.
So watch the thought and its ways
with care. And let it spring from love,
born out of concern for all beings".

Buddha

Makes you likeable

When I was checking in for my Las Vegas to London flight the other day, I noticed that the ground stewardess at the counter looked a bit grumpy. I couldn't blame her; it can't be the easiest job, especially when customers are rude or irritable. I was determined to make this lady smile, just a little one would do. I knew that I needed to give her my sincere attention.

My turn came and I handed her my passport, put the suitcase on the scales, and saw that there was no conveyor belt between the scale and the one that takes the suitcase to the plane (like we have in Europe). After this incident I noticed that this is the case in many airports in the US. After weighing the suitcase, the stewardess had to lift the heavy suitcase by herself and put it manually on the conveyor belt behind her. So when she lifted my suitcase, I said: "Now I understand why you don't have a mirror behind you."

She turned around, half smiling, and asked: "What do you mean?"
"They didn't install a mirror because nobody wants to see that every time you turn around and put a suitcase on the conveyor belt, you give it the finger."

She couldn't stop laughing. Her colleagues looked at her sidelong with a hint of jealousy. Why couldn't they have a customer who'd make them laugh and smile? We talked and laughed for a while and the last thing she said to me was: "I gave you a free upgrade, so enjoy your flight and see you soon." I'm sure this incident brightened her day and I bet she shared the story with her colleagues later. By the way, her name was Dorris. So if you happen to be in Las Vegas International airport at Virgin Atlantic counters, please send her my warm regards.

The real secret is giving sincere attention without trying to get something from the other person in return. It is up to you! There's nothing more powerful than an act of Attention that aims only to let the other person know how much you appreciate them. It's like an arrow directly to the heart. Did I want something from this lady? Absolutely not. Although on second thoughts, yes. I wanted to make her smile; I wanted to do something for her, without expecting her to do something for me. I wanted her to feel good!

This is the fourth rule: Use your attention giving skills to help other people know and feel they are significant. I guarantee you that if you obey this rule, you will bring a lot more happiness into your life and the lives of others. It will bring you many more friends too, or I should say real friends.

This rule taught me to hear sincere appreciation from other people. It urges me to be open to the attention of people who recognize my own true worth. This is the rule that helps me avoid giving my attention to wrong people. And this is the rule that makes me likeable and significant in my own little world. It will do the same for you.

When I shared this important lesson in one of my trainings, one of the participants said: "I'm not as well-known as you so my appreciation for other people won't be accepted in the same way as yours."

Nonsense. Don't wait to implement this rule: it is immaterial whether you're famous or not. Work the magic of this rule and become likeable, all the time, everywhere, in every encounter you have.

It is human nature that when you meet people many of them will feel superior to you in some way. If you give them your authentic attention, recognize their significance, you will win their heart and thus find a way to build a sincere relationship.

On my travels, I grab any opportunity to shop. I recently visited a conference in Boca Raton in Florida. I had a short break and decided to go to the nearest shopping mall and take a 'discovery tour'. (I have four younger sisters and two daughters so no wonder I love shopping!) US shopping malls are huge compared to the ones we have in Europe and after a while my feet started to hurt. So I sat down to relax and do some people-watching.

One of the mall's security team was standing in front of me; he was young, skinny and very bored. I looked up at him and said: "You should be proud of yourself for being able to stand for so many hours every day." He looked at me and smiled. But I could hear pity in my voice.

Then another thought came to mind: "We're all looking for some quiet time for ourselves. Mine is mainly when I'm on a plane. No emails, no telephone calls. It's time for me to be with myself. But you," I said with enthusiasm, "every day you have 10 pure hours for yourself."

The young man opened his big brown eyes and looked directly at me. He was interested in what I'd just said. I continued: "You should buy yourself a portable recorder and talk to yourself every day. Capture your thoughts, capture your desires, capture your new ideas. Every evening when you get home, download the recording and type it out." I paused for a moment to underline what I was going to say next. "Please type it out, because then your thoughts and dreams will materialize and become your new reality." There was an arrested look in his eyes. I'd planted a new hope in him by paying a little attention and showing him his significance. Then I gave him my business card. "Here are my contact details. When you've made it, please share your story with me. I want to know that you follow your dreams."

Using your giving attention skills can make other people feel significant. It will open doors in your business and in personal life. And it is all up to you!

Motivates you and others around you

When you are motivated your ability to give attention to other people naturally increases. The opposite is also true – if you pay attention to other people you increase their motivation as well as your own.

I've always opposed giving prizes or rewards as a way of motivating people to perform well. If you want these people to pay attention to the task – especially when it's about helping others – the lure of a prize will diminish their attention to the ones they're supposed to be helping.

How many times have you heard this: 'It's not about you, your company, your products or your services. It's about meeting customer needs and adding value'? Think about it: do you like to be sold? An attempt to sell me insults my intelligence and wastes my time. Now ask yourself this question, do you like to be helped? Most reasonable people do.

It seems that attention (and the motivation of others) doesn't respond very well to commands. 'Buy this!' 'Pay attention!' and all those other orders are a huge turn-off. But people do respond to clear questions that take care of their needs. Questions like 'what do you think about this?' or 'how would you improve it?' work well.

So, if you want to increase your motivation and the motivation of others, the answer may be using the right question.

Giving authentic attention to others gives you the opportunity to communicate, engage, solve their problems, educate and share knowledge with them and even add value to their business. Nobody likes to be told what to do or to feel that they are being sold something. We like to be consulted about our ideas, wants and needs. Nowadays it is wiser to make suggestions to other people and let them act upon their own conclusions.

Many people fail to make sales because they think they know what the customer needs and urge them to buy it. Selling becomes a lot easier when you pay sincere attention to your customers, when you ask them to share their ideas with you. It makes them feel that it was their idea to buy your product or service. You won't need to sell them because they will instantly cooperate with you and buy.

It is all up to you! Creating, connecting with other people or expanding business relationships is not about selling – it's about value creation without selling, while establishing trust, confidence and belief. Trust me when I tell you that your existing and potential clients have heard it all before.

If you do the right thing and put your customer's needs first you will generate more revenue much faster than ever before. When you start paying more attention to your customer's needs then your revenue will grow. You'll soon find you no longer have a revenue problem to complain about.

This ability to motivate others around you and help them feel they are implementing their own ideas works just as well in your personal life. Take for example my family. When my dear wife and I want to go shopping or do other domestic chores, we always ask our daughters to schedule where they want to go, while also planning time for the chores. They act as our tourist guides for the day. Guess what – we achieve much more, have a lot of fun and there are no arguments.

I hope you now understand that it is all up to you and that you've also learned the importance of giving attention as a way of motivating others to cooperate with you. So what will you do differently today?

SECRET #5: INGREDIENT X

"Where attention goes energy flows."

James Redfield

Gets you noticed

The fact that attention is still unknown territory and is one of the most intensely studied topics in psychology and cognitive neuroscience make it very attractive and somewhat mysterious... A little like the secret formula of Coca-Cola.

We can't stand self-centered people who are so involved with themselves that they can't pay attention to us. We want someone to tune into our mental 'talk show', not their own. Do you really think that your own issues and concerns are so important? It is time to wake up and change.

While studying in law school I found that every student could get extra bonus points at the end of the semester for productive participation in the classroom. I was not a great talker in those days, but I still got those bonus points. How? Do you want to know the secret? Let me share it with you.

I decided to find out how the professor awarded these bonus points. I was surprised to discover that as he didn't remember the students' names, at the end of the semester he'd look at all their identity cards (which had a photo of the student on them) and give bonus points to the faces he remembered. He assumed that if he remembered a face, that person must have participated in class. Fair assumption. Knowing that, I decided to use what I now call my sincere attention skills to listen carefully every time another student participated.

Naturally, the professor noticed that and rewarded me with bonus points at the end of the semester. My sincere attention got me noticed and instantly rewarded!

The same is true when a teacher pays attention to his students.

At one point in my corporate career, I taught tax law at five universities as well as working my regular job. I did it because I liked listening to my students' stories. I acted as a mentor and coach many times. This behaviour got me noticed by the students and many of them asked the faculty if they could take my classes. My rating at a lecturer was driven by my ability to give authentic attention to my students. It's a lesson that's stayed with me, and I practice it every time I give a keynote to an audience.

What about the work environment? If you are an employer isn't it obvious that the more you give sincere attention to your employees, the more they notice you and reward you with hard work and reliability. As you may know, the number one reason employees change jobs is not money, its appreciation. They want their employer to recognize their hard work and give them sincere positive attention.

I learned this early on in my corporate career. When I was acting Managing Director of a global financial firm, we established a new project called: 'This is my idea!' We encouraged all of the firm's employees, from all over the world and from different departments, to come up with ideas to improve the company's performance, ones that would simplify their work. I remember one example from a post lady based in India. Every day she had to make two trips to the local post office, which was a 45 minute walk each way, copy the list of packages and post that arrived, go back to the office, type it up, and go back to the post office to send the post.

She suggested buying a fax machine (this was before the days of email) so she could send the list to the post office and confirm it by fax. It was a simple idea but it saved a lot of time and manpower. When we implemented it, her boss waited until she'd left for the day before putting a sticker on her computer screen (it was called a 'sparky' because it was shaped like a light bulb). Then he put a brightly wrapped gift – a TV or CD player – on her desk where she and her co-workers would see it as soon as they got into work the next morning. The 'This is my idea' initiative repaid the firm with much more than ideas, it also gave it more hard working and committed employees and a happier environment to work in. Which companies and people stand out and get noticed? It's definitely the ones who listen carefully and pay attention to grousing and complaints, even when they're irritating. These people and companies do not want to lose out on the opportunity to get closer to another human being and are flexible enough to change their way of doing things if necessary. They know that this is the only way to get noticed and make a difference. If they won't do it, a competitor will.

We live in the age of attention scarcity and many people think it's hard to get attention. They are hungry for attention and long to get noticed, but how? As we have already learned, they have it the wrong way round. It is not getting attention that will attract others to you (or your company, products or services); it is GIVING authentic attention that draws others in like a magnet. But what makes it hard for a lot of people is the fact that 'attention' is almost like an unknown ingredient. If they knew what 'attention' was, they would surely give more of it, with sincerity. Then they'd get noticed for all the right reasons.

Do you think I've lost my mind? Of course I know that idiots get attention, but I'm afraid the idiot will be noticed in a negative way. Lots of us will reward him with attention (probably the negative kind), but there are very few who will reward this idiot with positive attention, such as friendship or business opportunities.

Next time you see someone receiving attention and praise, you'll know that it isn't down to luck. Giving undivided attention is the first and most vital ingredient in any relationship. It will get you noticed. It is impossible to communicate, much less bond, with someone who can't or won't focus on you. Getting noticed depends on your ability to give attention to others. If you work at it, you will receive plenty of praise and acknowledgement and that feels wonderful!

Turns you into a leader

I want you to think about the last time you helped somebody. Did this person accept your help? Or maybe he doubted your intentions? Do you think that the tendency of this person to accept or refuse your help influences the kind of relationship you have with them?

Helping is another way of giving attention to another person. As I mentioned in the Introduction, the quality of the 'attention' you give to another is not affected by their decision to accept or refuse it. On the other hand, if the two of you have a close relationship, he is more likely to listen and act upon your suggestions. Thus, the more your attention is accepted by the other person, the more leadership abilities you will develop.

Back in 2001, John Beck and Thomas Davenport, published their landmark book 'The Attention Economy'. Their hypothesis is that in this era of Continuous Partial Attention (CPA), brands need to focus on consumer attention as the ultimate currency in the marketplace. In the Attention Economy, thought leaders must focus on gaining Share of Mind to attain the top-of-mind trusted advisor position. The more you gain knowledge and understanding about this unknown ingredient called 'attention', the more you will be able to lead your market.

As a leader, of your company, your family, your own life, you need to be an expert in attention management. This is not an easy task, I know. As a leader, your ability to give attention to other people will direct their attention to what you want them to focus on. I believe this is the key for any leader nowadays. (More about it in the bonus chapter of my limited addition of my book dealing with 'Attentional Leadership'.)

As you've noticed I always like to share my personal stories in my presentations, trainings and right here in this book. Why? Did you know that a story is one of the most powerful ways to capture people's attention? Understanding this helped me realize why those stories lit up my brain and this realization was enough to direct me down a new path for the next seven years.

If you want to give people your attention and motivate positive action, here are four techniques that work:

i. **Tell a story**: Story-telling is the oldest technique for sharing information. People like to listen to good stories. Good stories trigger emotional responses in the listener and open their brain to receive more information. This information is likely to be remembered because stories are easier to recall than a list of facts.

ii.   **Give them a great purpose**: If you want people to engage with you try giving them a higher purpose. Naturally most people's attention is on themselves, so they miss a lot of the things going on around them. When you show people how their abilities and actions can make a difference in other people's lives, you actually give their action a higher purpose. That will spark their interest and help them to become more motivated, committed, and more willing to contribute to others.

iii.   **Create an unexpected event:** People's attention switches on immediately when something unexpected happens. Engaging their curiosity means they wake up, pay closer attention and look for solutions. The excitement zone always supports brain alertness.

iv.   **Be an attention magnet:** Attention attracts attention. If you want to capture someone's attention, give your own first. People mirror other people's behaviour. Your ability to pay full authentic attention will automatically stimulate others to pay attention to you. This is an incredibly powerful tool for motivating other people's positive attention. Remember, attention is the only thing you really have to give to another person. So switch it on and light others up.

Unfortunately there are many negative ways to capture people's attention too. We are constantly exposed to negative information and negative people. But if you want to win someone's full attention, only positive strategies really work.

PART TWO

Be Authentic
and
Pay Attention

"No one can succeed
and remain successful
without the
friendly cooperation
of others."

Napoleon Hill

CHAPTER 3

THE 7C FUNDAMENTAL ELEMENTS OF ATTENTION

"Since you cannot
do good at all,
you are to pay special attention
to those who,
by the accidents of time,
or place, or circumstances,
are brought into closer
connection with you."

Saint Augustine

CHAPTER 3: THE 7C FUNDAMENTAL ELEMENTS OF ATTENTION

SEVEN FUNDAMENTAL ELEMENTS

Congratulations on making it this far. I hope you're enjoying discovering the nuts and bolts of 'Giving Attention' and all of the building-blocks that will help you create sincere and authentic long-lasting relationships.

Attention is king in the new economy. Your success will be determined by your ability to give sincere attention to other people, be it your clients, suppliers, colleagues, friends, family members, strangers, but also to yourself.

Giving attention and maintaining your customers' interest is a huge problem today. How many times have you walked into a restaurant or store and nobody gave attention to you? Worse than that maybe they didn't even acknowledge you? A great and authentic relationship-builder knows how to give his sincere attention to others.

Here are the seven fundamental elements you need to follow to succeed at the art of giving attention and developing authentic relationships in all spheres of your life. They will allow you to fulfill your dreams and desires.

ELEMENT#1: COOPERATION

Everyday, we spend a lot of time talking to other people. Despite social networking and digital technologies, most of the time we still communicate face-to-face. Communication relies on cooperation.

We are expected to cooperate by dedicating our mental energy toward processing the messages received from the other person. This cooperation is the basic element of attention and it is called 'Paying Attention.'

Are you listening to me?
What do you hear right now?

I am currently at home. I hear the sound of the fridge working, the goat in the small farm outside, the humming sound of my neighbour's car. Did you have similar answers to me? Did you notice that it was a tricky question?

To answer this question, you had to shift your attention and take control of your sensory experience. You weren't just hearing; you were listening and describing what you heard. You experienced the difference between hearing and listening – and that's what attention is.

Let's imagine you are at a crowded party; everyone is talking and laughing, there are no quiet corners anywhere. Your auditory system will be working hard to help you control the sounds around you. It will filter out most of the sounds unless you need to notice them – imagine a lady suddenly shouting "Help! Help!" Your auditory system will be on red alert; you'll instantly tune into her cries and your attention will kick in.

One of the basic elements of giving your attention to others is by listening to what they say, not just hearing them. Listening – really taking in what other people say – forms an immediate connection and the other person will be far more willing to cooperate with you. Hearing is a natural process (unless you suffer some genetic or developmental problem or have had an accident that affects your hearing), but listening is a skill that we're in danger of losing in a world of digital distraction and information overload.

You can hear a lot of noises around you, but you have to choose which noise to attend to. In other words, a lot of people (as well as things) can trigger our senses and will try to force themselves on us (also via social media and online), but we choose who can enter our attention space and whom we want to give attention to. We show that by active listening.

However, listening alone does not mean that you are fully paying attention. Let me give you an example.

Have you ever lost your concentration while talking to someone and allowed your thoughts to drift off to other projects? In that moment, can we say that you were still paying some sort of attention to the other person? Probably yes, in your subconscious mind, but you were certainly not listening.

Stop thinking 'what will I say next?' instead of being there in that moment with the other person. When you listen to them, people will be happy to cooperate with you since you are already cooperating with them. Remember what we discovered earlier? How people like to reward those who pay authentic attention to them?

If you are interested in having more effective cooperation with others, listen to them first. Listen to their ideas, opinions, needs and desires; it will definitely serve you in building your relationship with them. If you listened to your client and heard that he reads his emails only in the morning and evening, you'll know in future the best time to email him and get his attention. Simple? Yes, it is. But many people lose valuable cooperation opportunities because they don't listen, they don't pay attention. You need to listen ALL THE TIME, because how can you know when they are going to say something that could be useful or important to you?

People want to be recognized, they want others to pay attention to them and respect them. One of the best ways to do it is by authentic active listening. I call this 'aural persuasion'. By listening to the other person, you're actually sending them the message that they are significant to you and that you appreciate them. If you sincerely behave this way EVERYBODY will be happy to cooperate with you as they will also get a boost. No-one forgets a good listener.

When you were a child did your parents or teachers ever say "Please pay attention when I am talking to you"? I bet they didn't get your attention or your cooperation!

Worse than that, some of us learned to ignore this request. That's because they were demanding your attention and, as we have already seen, attention-grabbing just doesn't work long-term.

When I was younger I only used to give my attention to things I thought were important. I used only to listen to people who were important to me, be it my parents, teachers, boss, or my army commander (I didn't have much choice in this case). It was a mistake. The people I didn't listen to turned their backs on me and I regret that to this day.

Why didn't I listen? It seems to me that the reality we are living in makes it difficult for us to decide whether or not to listen to someone. We probably demand too much immediate return on our attention investment in the other person. Operating in this way damages our ability to give sincere attention to every person, which is the basic ingredient of healthy cooperation between human beings.

The real power of 'WE'

Why do I need to talk about the importance of cooperation in communication, isn't it just common sense? Unfortunately it isn't. If you look around, you'll find many people participating in teamwork trainings. Companies pay enormous amounts of money to achieve better teamwork in the workplace. Companies see 'teamwork' and cooperation between colleagues as one of their core values. Why?

The 'Us' against 'Them' mentality is widespread in society. In many of my trainings I use a simple exercise to emphasize this point. It works flawlessly in every country I do it. Surprising? Not really. Ever since our childhood we've heard: "Go get them", "Watch your back," and other such expressions. The problem starts when our culture teaches us to focus our attention on right-wrong thinking. This creates strong mental habits which govern our thinking as well as our actions. Even in our most loving and trusting relationships, we often end up playing good-bad/right-wrong games.

The good news is that you can unlearn this approach and start giving more authentic attention to other people in your life. As a consequence you will begin to have more genuine cooperation in your professional and personal life. Authentic attention will guide you to the power of 'We'.

ELEMENT#2: CONSISTENCY

> "Success is neither magical
> nor mysterious.
> Success is the natural
> consequence of consistently
> applying basic fundamentals."
>
> Jim Rohn

The second law in Deepak Chopra's bestselling book 'The Seven Spiritual Laws of Success' is the Law of Giving and Receiving. He says: "The universe operates through constant and dynamic exchange... giving and receiving are different aspects of the same flow of energy in the universe. In our willingness to give that which we seek, we keep the abundance of the universe circulating in our lives."

Practicing the Law of Giving and Receiving is simple – it is all about consistency and reciprocity. If you want attention and appreciation, you need to give attention and appreciation to others. You need to learn to give attention to others all the time, not only on special occasions or when you feel like it. Giving attention consistently is a very important element of giving attention.

Practice creates skill

Why is consistency an important element of paying attention? I can think of two main reasons. One, consistency is a clear sign of authenticity.

Only a person who makes giving attention an integral part of her personality will be perceived by others as real and sincere. The second reason is that consistency and regular practice will build your skills and you will be able to give attention to others more naturally, more often, in more effective and efficient ways.

People who are good at building relationships tend to consistently give attention to others. If you want to build sincere and long-lasting relationships you need to give attention in a reliable and predictable manner, supported by mental energy that flows in an even and consistent way.

Here are some strategies that will help you consistently give attention in every interaction.

i.   Monitor factors that disturb your attention. Maybe you find it harder to concentrate at different times of the day? Or perhaps feelings like anxiety, fear or sadness cause your focus to waver. If you're due to meet someone for the first time, make sure that it happens in a place you'll both find comfortable.

ii.   Become aware of the times when you give attention to others in the most consistent way. Encourage yourself, at least at the beginning, to use these times of sufficient mental energy to focus on building relationships with others.

iii.   Learn from great attention givers. Use them as role models to encourage your own attention consistency.

iv.   Learn new strategies that you can use in your daily practice to advance the consistency of your attention giving and relationship-building capabilities. This book and my training courses can help here.

Consistent attention = strong client relationship

I assume that by now you understand the role excellent attention giving plays in building relationships. You know that building strong relationships with others requires a consistent and ongoing effort to retain their hard-won loyalty. The importance of consistency in your attention to others is huge, since other people want to have confidence that you'll deliver on your promises every time, not just when it's convenient.

If you consistently deliver authentic attention to others, you (and your company) can grow and reach extraordinary heights. It won't guarantee success but it will lay the foundation for you to achieve more. It will distinguish you from your competitors too.

Who do you consider a real friend: somebody who's always there for you or somebody you hear from once a year when he sends you a birthday card? Consistency of attention creates strong relationships.

I recently bought a product online. All the testimonials helped the product look and sound great, on the surface. The company's marketing spiel said: "We care about you, every client at a time!" It was a different story once I'd bought their product. It takes days to get a response from the support department, and that's if they respond at all. "We care about you" seems to be an empty promise.

Can you guess how I feel about this company now? Is the company building a strong customer relationship with me? They do not even attempt to pay attention to me! I am just another client. Those of us who run sizeable businesses know firsthand that building customer loyalty takes time. It's an ongoing task that can make the difference between success and failure. And consistency in every area plays a key role, including paying sincere attention to your loyal clients.

Is consistent attention giving to your spouse, children or friends also beneficial? Absolutely.

Your spouse wants to think that they know you inside-out and that includes your behaviour. Inconsistency in behaviour, feelings and attention-giving can destroy a couple's relationship. Sudden changes, including a change in the amount of sincere attention you give to your partner, cause suspicion and doubt and could end up destroying the trust in your relationship. You have to avoid this if you want to maintain a stable relationship. My advice to you: give attention to your spouse spontaneously, be surprising, be impulsive, but be all of these things consistently.

The other day I had lunch with a very interesting friend of mine. He is currently the CEO of well-known multinational. We've implemented many of the ideas I'm sharing in this book within his company. The results are amazing. We've spent a lot of time discussing consistency and paying attention as key elements in building strong relationships. After listening carefully and giving me his input and ideas, he challenged me to come up with three tips to help a person (or a company) maintain consistency while giving attention to others. Here they are:

1.   Create opportunities to give your attention to others – listen carefully to other people's needs and problems and try to discover solutions with them.
2.   Invite your contacts and people you met recently to give their feedback on the meetings and what you could improve.

3.   Follow-up and follow through. After you meet people for the first time, make sure that you follow up and continue giving them your constant attention.

The more consistent you are with these actions, the better you will be at building relationships. Generally, people will only want you in their network if you are genuine, give authentic attention and provide value.

ELEMENT#3: CREDIBILITY

> "The value of a man should be seen
> in what he gives and not in what
> he is able to receive."
>
> Albert Einstein

Let your name ~~walk~~ run ahead of you

If you want to see real results from giving attention to other people, you need to be credible. Credibility should be the basis of any interaction and relationship with another person.

How do you judge other people? How do you decide if you like and trust somebody? If you know somebody is not credible do you pay attention to him? Your authentic ability to give attention to other people will make you be likeable and build their trust – this will give you all the credibility you need. There is a direct link between your giving attention skills and your credibility.

The opposite is also true. If you are uninterested in other people, or if you do not show your interest in the right way, people will trust and like you less. You will be considered less credible in the market.

During my corporate career I was able to create trust with new clients while we were still at the negotiating stage just because I'd developed a special bond with them. Guess how? Simply by giving my attention to them, also outside of the deal itself. My genuine interest led to me being introduced to a lot of new clients and, by consistently giving attention to them, they liked and trusted me, which instantly boosted my credibility.

Don't think "hey if I give attention to other people, they'll automatically like me and believe everything I say" or you'll get disappointed very fast! It takes time to build trust, people don't give it the first time you pay them attention. But one thing is sure, your sincerity in paying attention to others will give you an edge and will guide the other person to count you as credible. They will be far more likely to believe you and your message.

Many years ago, during my work at a leading wealth management group, my boss sent me to Switzerland to visit a very wealthy family which was a prospective client. My boss knew something I did not understand myself, that I was probably the most likely member of our team to fulfill this mission, to persuade this family to become a new client.

I arrived at Zurich and a driver in an old black limousine picked me up from the airport. The drive took about 40 minutes. We arrived at the gate of the property and then had to drive for another 10 minutes before we reached the house, or castle. They lived in a huge old castle! A servant led me to a large room where I found the head of the family, a very interesting man of 82, and his daughter and son. We sat down and talked for about four hours. We talked about everything, my background, the castle's history, the history of the family, and politics. It was fascinating and I spent most of the conversation listening rather than talking.

It was getting late and after lunch we moved to a side room, where tea and cookies were served (my weak point). I realized that I had to leave for the airport within an hour, but we hadn't discussed business yet! Finally I gathered my courage, looked directly at the old man and asked: "Can we discuss business now?"

His face went red. He looked at his daughter, then his son before looking back at me. His voice was shaking when he said: "Isn't it obvious that it is with you, my son?" This was the first time I'd realized the power of giving attention and the way your authenticity can build credibility.

Pump up the value!

You create real value for other people by paying attention to them. But paying attention will also teach you how to create value for them. You can pump up your own value by using an introduction from a mutual friend or acquaintance. It helps you stand out from other people who also want to gain access to this person.

Let's say the other person is a potential client. If you learn about their needs by sincerely listening to them, being with them, and helping them, do you really think you need to pitch to them? You have already created value in their minds.

Let's take the last example further. Once you give authentic attention to another, this person is more likely to share valuable information with you, higher quality information than they would share with others. Now can you understand the edge you'll gain over other people simply by being authentic?

It may be simple, but it was revolutionary for me. Many clients chose to work with me, not because I was the best international tax lawyer in the world (I'm not!), but because I gave them more value – I listened to their emotional needs, I connected them with others, I shared information on different subjects.

Over the years, people close to me have warned me not to share everything I know with everybody I meet. But guess what? I can't stop doing it. But these days I understand what I developed during those years – a personality that others found valuable.

What have you got to be scared of? You are the only person in the world who can be YOU. People know that when they choose you, you will deliver what they value the most, whether they are practical or emotional benefits. The valuable experience you give to others during your interactions, the excitement, energy, and enthusiasm, creates your credible personality. They believe you will continue creating this special feeling in them every time the two of you get together. And they will cherish it forever.

I want to share something with you that I've never shared with anybody before. Please don't think I'm saying it to impress you! I've always been keen to understand why other people liked me. Why would someone I'd met for the first time feel almost instantly that I can add value to them?

The older I got, the more I felt that people saw me as a conscientious human being, someone who really cared about them. That's helped me grow emotionally as well as broadening my social networks. Of course, this directly affected the way other people see me today: as a likeable personality who can substantially increase their value. I am honoured that people feel like this about me.

Build it before you need it

It takes time to be valuable to others and to really feel you have value to share with them. Moreover, you can only gain other people's trust little by little over time. So why do some people approach us and give us their attention only when they need us?

The other day I got an email via LinkedIn from a businessman I'd met seven years ago. We'd only met once, but it was a great meeting and we connected instantly. I kept in touch but never got a reply. Suddenly he 'found' me and wanted to meet for coffee. I was relieved, I'd been waiting for our follow up meeting for a long time, finally he's made time for me... Please excuse my cynicism. After checking the business news, I found out that his recent company had filed for bankruptcy.

As an authority in the business relationship world, I know that you must give value to others and build relationships with them long before you need anything from them. You start giving your sincere attention to other people as soon as possible.

If you want other people to consider you as a valuable and credible person, start connecting with them today. Build value over time, there are no shortcuts. There is nothing wrong in targeting specific people or a specific audience. You do not need to be, and you never will be, a valuable person to everybody in the universe. So why not reach out to the people you want to give your attention to?

Eventually, there will be more people who see your personal value and believe in you. Your circle of true friends will increase. These are the people you want to give your authentic attention to.

So what are you waiting for? Start today. Make a list of all the people you know, think of how you can help them, approach them and start working on sharing your value with them and giving them your full attention.

You need to constantly think – how can I create, on a regular basis, the network of people or the community that I want to share my ideas, thoughts and attention with? Trust me; the time will come when you will be so valuable for each one of these people that they will want to be around you. The more people you know and give your authentic attention to, the more valuable you will be to them (and to yourself!) Consequently more opportunities will come your way, helping you toward success.

You need to understand that your potential to connect with other people and give them your attention is far greater than what you've implemented so far. Go and get those opportunities, do not let them pass you by. Please, please do not wait to give your attention to other people. And definitely don't do it only when you need them because that's the fastest way to turn people off.

Build a community of people who value you the way you are, before you need them. Because when and if you need them, they will be there waiting to help and support you.

ELEMENT#4: COMMUNICATION

> "The most important thing in communication is hearing what isn't said."
>
> Peter Drucker

The unspoken language

It's incorrect to assume that talking is an active mode of communication while paying attention and listening is passive. Phrases like 'shut up and listen' show that we do not really understand the power of listening and giving attention.

Did you know that effective listening and paying full attention is much more demanding on our brain than talking? I often feel exhausted after an intense conversation or meeting. Why? Because giving sincere attention demands real concentration which consumes a lot of mental energy. You need to concentrate; you need to be in the moment, you need to be fully engaged in the meaning of the words that the other person is saying.

You do not need to master every active listening technique. I propose you choose the ones that are most comfortable and natural to you and go master them. You will be surprised how interesting conversations become. The other person will enjoy the conversation as well and you will understand each other more, without you needing to say a single word.

Answer these three easy questions to find out if you listen to others and show them that you really are paying attention:

i.   Do you ask the other person a question and wait for their answer?

ii.   How do you respond to questions asked by the other person? Fast and direct?

iii.   How does the other person show they know you are listening and paying attention to them?

If you can answer all of these questions properly congratulations! You are a great communicator and well on the way to understanding the quality of your attention skills.

If you want to improve your communication skills you must be self-aware. How can you effectively communicate with others if you don't know yourself, your strengths and abilities, weaknesses and communication style? Giving attention is a delicate and influential art. To have the ability to make others feel understood you need to be authentic. Self awareness is one key to authentic attention.

Two-way street

How do you know when somebody is paying attention to what you have said? I bet you know how to answer this question!

Research from around the world shows that everyone can, to a certain degree, visually assess other people's level of listening. The signs aren't obvious, but you know what to look for: the other person maintains eye contact with you, or they nod, they face you, they are silent when you speak (during a telephone call you may have to ask them if they're still there), or they occasionally make short responses like 'hmm' or 'I see'. Of course, every culture has its own nuances, but overall these are good examples.

As a side note, I should mention that during our communication with others we pay attention to their visual expressions in order to understand what they mean.

When I'm on stage I use hand gestures to convey my message more clearly. You can probably pick up what the other person is feeling by watching their facial expressions, right? Another interesting phenomenon is that our perception of sounds is affected by the visual input we receive. This is called McGurk Effect. But your eyes are not entirely necessary when you're paying attention to others (see the telephone example).

If you and the person you are paying attention to have the same background, or both of you understand 'attention' in the same way, you should be pretty good at reading each other's non-verbal signals. But if you come from different cultures the signals we use to perform giving attention, such as eye contact, can mean something different to them. That makes communication more complex.

Different cultures often have different ways of paying attention. Knowing that will help you understand the other person and become a better communicator.   These cultural differences can have serious consequences.

I once worked with a very gentle and quiet lady, who was originally from the Far East. I used to chat with her once in while, even though we didn't work in the same department. One day, she entered my office with red eyes.

"What happened?" I asked.
"I got fired."

I invited her to sit down, gave her a glass of water and closed the door. I learned that she'd got fired because her boss claimed she did not pay attention to him when he talked to her. But she insisted that she'd always listened to him.

I don't remember the details any more, but could this misunderstanding have been caused by cultural differences? In some cultures, looking into somebody's eyes means you're paying attention to them, but in others making direct eye contact with somebody who is superior to you is seen as defiance. By the way, I didn't know this at the time I was working for that company. Maybe if I'd known it then I could have helped this lady get her job back.

Sometimes during meetings with people from different cultural backgrounds than my own I sense that they are not paying attention to me. Sometimes they're not. But what if I've made a wrong judgment and they actually were listening to me? If it ever happens to you ask the other person a question related to what you have just talked about. Then you will be able to find out if they were paying full attention rather than listening with their mind elsewhere.

There are three important steps to becoming a great communicator by paying attention.

i.   You need to understand the significance of attention giving and active listening.
ii.   You need to be eager to learn more about 'attention' (for example by reading this book and attending one of our seminars and trainings).
iii.   You need to go out there and practice your attention skills.

Here is my guarantee – showing that you're paying attention will improve your communication at home, at work and with every person you interact with.

ELEMENT#5: CARING

"Kindness in words creates confidence.
Kindness in thinking
creates profoundness.
Kindness in giving creates love."

Lao Tzu

Respect the dignity of others

Do you genuinely care about other people? Without authentic care and interest, you'll find it an uphill battle to uncover opportunity and gain new business. I want you to understand how critical this element is for building relationships – the only way to build a relationship based on trust is to respect the other person's dignity. By paying YOUR authentic attention to others, you respect their dignity and really show that you care about them.

There's a great story about a young guy who approached an old Rabbi and challenged him to explain the secret of his life. The young man asked the old man if he could teach him everything he knew in the time that he was able to balance on one foot (a metaphor for a short time). The old man replied: "What is hateful to yourself, do not do to your fellow man. This is the whole secret; the rest is just commentary. Go and study it."

This story resembles the Golden Rule or ethic of reciprocity which essentially states: 'One should treat others as one would like others to treat oneself.' It seems like common sense, but as you've probably heard before, common sense is not common anymore. If you treat others with respect, if you care about other people's needs and desires, if you pay attention to them with all your heart then they will do the same for you.

Once, after changing jobs and feeling very despondent, I did some soul-searching. I wanted to find the one main motivator that makes me who I am. I noticed during my corporate career, during my times of success and failure, that my greatest asset was my ability to care and interact with a wide variety of people from different countries, different cultures, and different backgrounds. That's made me one of the global leading authorities on relationship-building and networking. I probably care a little bit more and from a deeper place than other people. I really do care for everybody, even strangers in the street. I am always moved by others' suffering. I am firmly connected to that inner core of caring.

If you are a businessperson or a professional, you may be thinking: 'that's great for you Itzik, but this is not for me. I am a professional. It does not work in business.' You're wrong. I am also a professional. I'm not trying to convince you to be self-indulgent or sentimental; I just want you to understand that when you give Authentic Attention to another person you really need to care. Caring comes from within. You need to be brave enough to use it and enjoy it.

Queenly caring

The next question should be how do I care? Start by putting yourself in the other person's shoes. Other people are living and breathing creatures too. They have their family and friends. They have successes and failures. They have emotions. They also want to succeed. They want somebody to pay attention to them, listen to them, and care about their story, exactly like you do. So go give it to them, what are you waiting for?

Why do I insist that you start showing you care for others now? I've learned over the years that caring for other people and making them feel important is rarely achieved by one single gesture. Not even by a few major ones. Caring is a process that demands a lot of small touches over time. So that is why I want you to start this process NOW.

As I watch the TV coverage of the King and Queen of the Netherlands and their recent German visit, I can't help wondering why so many Dutch people prefer the Queen to the King. What makes her so different? Suddenly, as I watched the programme, I saw it.

The couple were leaving their hotel and walking to the car. Camera crews and journalists had been waiting for the royal couple to come out. The King was the first to exit and his attention went directly to the journalists. Then the Queen left the hotel, but she did something else. She took a few seconds to say something to the doorman. You could see the warmth on her face as she looked at him, the caring and sincere attention she gave him. You did not need to hear anything. Now, imagine if you were this doorman; wouldn't you go home and tell your family and friends? I'm sure you'd cherish this moment for the rest of your life.

Employee of the month

The same applies in the work environment. If you want your employees to feel that you care about them, then take the time to understand their needs. They will naturally work harder for the company and give their utmost to help it achieve its goals. How do you show your employees you care? By showing constant attention to every one of them.

One of my clients is a large international Indian group. Last year, I visited their headquarters. I know the company has several thousand employees, but in the offices I visited there was only one floor. "So where did you hide the rest of your staff?" I asked the CEO.
He laughed and said: "You tell us all the time that we need to show our caring to our employees. But how will we be able to really show it to each employee if all of them are in the same building? That's one of the reasons we decided to have a few separate offices with a maximum of 200 people in each one. It cost us a bit more, but we retain most of our employees. So in the long run it works out well financially. It gives us the possibility to give attention to each of our employees on a regular basis. Our employees don't just see we care, they feel we really do. That makes them stay with us."

I loved it. This great way of thinking allowed this company to become one of the largest in its sector globally. This attention-giving created a culture of respect and open communication. It helped the employer to care for his employees and helped the employees care for their employer.

Lack of appreciation and personal recognition is one of the main reasons people change jobs. It's important for a worker to feel that their employer cares about them and pays attention to them. When I went to our local supermarket the other day I saw a poster of the employee of the month on the wall behind the cashier. Great initiative? It could be. It's one way of thanking the winning employee each month and letting your clients and upper management know about that individual's accomplishments. But in this case the poster was stained and looked like it was about to fall off the wall. It must have been there for ages. Sad. It was actually serving in the opposite way – it looked as though this employer did not really care about his employees.

It's okay to say it

Has anyone ever asked you 'do you need some attention?' or said 'you have all my attention'? There's nothing wrong in approaching people and showing you care by explicitly telling them that you're going to give them your attention. Would you refuse if somebody gave you a precious gift? There's no bigger gift than showing a person you care by giving them a part of yourself – your attention.

Furthermore, when you give somebody else the commitment and time to listen, you also need to find a way to give value to them. How can you help them? What can you do for them? Stating your value is a very important part of the attention you are giving to the other person.

When you say to somebody and really mean it: "You've got all my attention" it is a great act of caring. So stick with it and keep your commitment. Please don't start checking your mobile phone! Be there in that moment, be with that person fully.

ELEMENT#6: CREATIVITY

*"The essence of all art
is to have pleasure
in giving pleasure."*

Dale Carnegie

At first glance, it looks as though 'creativity' and 'paying attention' are two contradictory concepts. Some may mistakenly think that the mind wanders freely in the creative process, but when you pay attention you need to be focused. Being creative is actually another act that takes intense focus from both the conscious and subconscious parts of the mind. I believe that creativity is a significant element in the act of paying attention. Let me explain.

Don't swim in a sea of sameness

There is no one concept of 'paying attention' that fits all people and there never will be. Every attention you give to another human being should be tailor-made, unique, special. Otherwise, it's not authentic attention; it is 'mass' attention – attention that you find in the sea of sameness.

Let's take an example. Two friends of yours have their birthday on the same day and they decide to celebrate it together. You're invited to the party and you need to buy a present for each of them. To make the example a bit more colourful, let's assume that one's male and one's female. Would you buy them both the same present or would you think carefully about their likes and dislikes and give each of them a present they may actually want? If you choose the first option, you're being lazy or need to understand the concept of 'paying attention' in more depth. If you really care about your friends, you'll be creative in your choice of gift. The more creative you are with regards to other people, the more you pay attention to them, then the more successful you will be in building long-lasting relationships.

118

If every person is unique, why not give every person unique attention? Everyone has different expectations and interests, so it stands to reason that they would probably have different preferences about how they are given attention. And we all have our own unique ways of giving attention to others. If you agree with these assumptions, you'll understand that the more you use your creativity in the process of giving attention to others, the more successful you will be because they'll remember you.

Why so? Feelings. If you give your attention to another person, it shows that you are interested in them. You will make the other person feel good, they'll remember you and what you said, and they'll be happy to build a relationship with you.

Creative attention

Robert Frost, the American poet, once said, "The brain is a wonderful organ. It starts working the moment it gets up in the morning and doesn't stop until it gets to the office." As you probably know, when you are busy at work there is no time for creative thoughts to pop into your head. I'm talking specifically about creative thoughts on how to connect with others. Thoughts that would attract clients, friends and partners.

Preparation helps you develop and nurture your creativity. Before I do a keynote presentation, I always prepare properly and talk, well in advance, with people from the relevant industry. I always pick up great ideas from these conversations that I can use in my presentation. This is 'Creative Attention' in action.

Do you prepare well in advance before you approach a potential client or before you meet a new person? Preparation can happen at any time, even during the meeting itself (for example, if your client shows you photos of his family), you can take in this new information and use it during the conversation to bond sincerely with the other person. This example of 'creative attention' can be used by anyone.

People may be struggling in these difficult times, so give them a pat on the back. Give them the attention they deserve. Try to find new ideas and ways to give REAL 'creative attention' to others.

Thus, you will shine and stand out from the crowd. They will see the difference between you and your competitors, but, even better than that, you will attract the clients who prefer your brand of 'creative attention'.

I believe that everyone and every company can find their own unique flavour of 'creative attention'. It's partly dependent on your personality but it's also something that everyone can develop, advance and improve.

ELEMENT#7: CHOICE

> "In a moment of decision
> the best thing you can do
> is the right thing.
> The worst thing you can do is nothing."
>
> Theodore Roosevelt

What are you giving your attention to right now? Whatever it may be it is, by definition, your highest priority. Only you decide on your priorities – so would you like to rethink your current choice?

We're bombarded by stimuli all the time, and, if we live in cities, we see so many people, maybe too many. If we were to pay attention to everybody and everything, we would quickly become overwhelmed and lose our energy. Possibly our sanity!

So, how do we decide what we want to give our attention to? How do we separate out those people who seem more important and/or relevant? Choice is the seventh basic element in giving authentic attention to others.

No choice but to pay attention!

I believe we can choose where to put our attention. You are in charge of that choice and should always be in the driver's seat. You are the one who gives your attention to another person, who listens to what they say and stops your mind wandering. In some situations it's very difficult to keep control of your attention. Practice helps. The fact that some choices are difficult to carry out is no reason to turn away from them.

Why is it important to make active choices about where we place our attention? WH Auden wrote: "Choice of attention – to pay attention to this and to ignore that – is to the inner life what choice of action is to the outer. In both cases a person is responsible for their choice and must accept the consequences."

When we choose to give our attention to another and build an authentic relationship, we encounter two challenges:

i.   The first challenge is distinguishing between essential,
        important people and people who do not deserve to get our
        attention, such as people who drain our energy.

ii.   The second is ensuring that our attention remains with that one
        specific person, rather than jumping to something else
        that grabs our attention.

How do we tackle these challenges? Two points of personal inquiry might bring you some insight:

•   Check with yourself if you are clear about what is important to
       you. Why? The answers to these questions can be significant
       reference points for choosing the right people to pay attention to.

•   When the potential for distraction arises, ask yourself what your
       motivation is when you follow that impulse rather than
       remaining with the person who matters.

One way or the other, the choice will be made and your attention will go somewhere. It's best if you make your choices yourself and choose who or what you want to give your attention to. This small decision can have a huge impact on your life and your success. Giving attention to others takes time; time is a scarce resource, so you'd better make a damn good choice!

Choose happiness

Sometimes we try to make ourselves happy by ignoring things. It doesn't work, of course. If you want to be happy, you're much better off learning to pay attention to things, especially the many good things that happen to you and the amazing people around you. If we choose to pay attention to something, we will understand it more fully and it will influence us more.

For some of us it is an easy choice while for others it isn't. One thing is certain, when you decide to pay attention to another person you've made a great choice. First, you've made a choice and are sticking with it. You're living consciously. Second, does anyone take the worst option if they've got a better one to choose instead? Of course not, since we always opt for the best choice. So if you made the right choice, the next feeling will naturally be happiness.

Make the right choice!

If we know how to make the right choices, we'll pay attention to the right people in our life and develop some great long-lasting relationships. But do we know how to make the right choices?

If we really wanted to find out every detail we'd need to go into a person's mind at the moment they make the choice and examine all the relevant parameters and the stimuli. The good news is that most people make their choices in a predictable way.

Let me show you how to choose whether to pay attention to somebody or not:

i.   Listen to what they are saying, interact with them.
ii.   Do you believe what they are saying? Yes or no?
iii.   Give this person a relationship value. What do I mean? Try to work out the possibility of building a relationship with this person in the long run. Will it work? What do you feel? Listen to the little voice within.

Only after you've followed the above three steps should you make the choice about whether to give your attention to this specific person. The whole process takes only seconds to carry out as most of it happens inside your head.

The time-management expert Alan Lakein recommends asking this insightful question several times a day – what is the most valuable use of my time right now? This question almost always has just one answer. That one thing is our highest priority and it deserves our full attention until the answer to the question changes. I suggest you ask similar questions when you are dealing with other people: who is the most valuable person that I can be giving my attention to right now?

I'm not talking about the most famous or important person in the room. At one company I worked for, my room was known as 'the wailing wall'. I wasn't part of HR, but many of my colleagues found my room to be a good place to come and open their hearts, to share, to get advice and leave with renewed energy and optimism. I loved listening to each person and helped as much as I could.

One day one of my colleagues had a very personal matter he needed help with so I closed my door to avoid us being disturbed. Fifteen minutes later the door opened and my boss, the CEO of the company, entered the room.

My colleague had just started crying and my boss wanted to know the reason why. Before my colleague could answer I politely asked my boss to leave. He didn't like it, but he had no other choice. I'd made a clear decision to give my sincere attention to my colleague and nobody was allowed to disturb it, not even my boss. Some of you may think 'big deal

Itzik, you did it when you were in a senior position at the company. I could never do that as I'd risk losing my job!' Do you really think so? Did you ever get fired from a company because you helped your colleagues? I doubt it! And if you were, be proud of it! I wouldn't want to work for a company that didn't respect its employees and their caring for each other. I had a lengthy discussion with my boss about this situation and after a while he respected my choice and sincerely embraced it as part of our company culture – the support colleagues should show each other at work.

I've used the above three step process in every interaction for at least the past five years, both in my business and personal life. This process saves me valuable time, but much more than that it allows me to be authentically and fully present in all of my interactions. It is one of the main reasons why I'm seen as a real Power Networker.

> "No one has ever
> become poor
> by giving."
>
> Anne Frank

THE ELEMENTS TAIL

Now you have read about the seven elements of authentic attention, it's time to ask yourself the following questions:

- Are you ready to affirm, commit and act on your commitment to give authentic attention to others?
- Do you really want to accomplish great things in life?
- Do you really want to connect with other people, learn about their passions, needs, life struggles, and business?
- Are you willing to work hard on your attention skills and develop your communication skills so you can improve your ability to get closer to others?

Whatever answers you give, you need to be committed. If you practice these seven basic elements of authentic attention™ every day, your life will soon be filled with great and magical moments.

Our attention is the source of all communication and connection with others. The only way for somebody to enter our minds and lives is for us to give them our authentic attention and thus invite them in. It's the basis for all genuine relationships, be they personal or professional.

Living our best and happiest lives, making our greatest possible contribution to the world, connecting and developing relationships with other people, these are all rooted in a simple habit: focusing our attention on those people who are most important to us. The choice about what and to whom we pay attention is fundamental to our future happiness and success. It creates our experience of reality.

"Pay attention
to your enemies,
for they are the first
to discover your mistakes."

Antisthenes

PART THREE

The Art of 'Attentional Networking™'

"There is no such thing
as a 'self-made' man.
We are made up
of thousands of others.
Everyone who has ever done
a kind deed for us,
or spoken one word
of encouragement to us,
has entered into the make-up
of our character and of our
thoughts,
as well as our success."

George Burton Adams

CHAPTER 4

ATTENTIONAL NETWORKING

"Non-cooperation with evil
is as much a duty
as is cooperation with good."

Mahatma Gandhi

CHAPTER 4: ATTENTIONAL NETWORKING

The Art of 'Attentional Networking'

She was an African lady in her fifties. Her family still lived in Africa. Every day I met her in the office at around 6pm, when she started her cleaning shift. I could smell her perfume as soon as she arrived as she always wore the same distinctive scent. Most of my colleagues had left already; I was one of the only ones to work late. In those days I worked as a commercial director for one of the largest banks in Europe.

She'd knock gently on my door to make sure she wasn't disturbing me. She always had the same positive energy and every day she'd greet me with a big smile. Her name was Olivia. Most days we'd chat for about 10-15 minutes on all kind of subjects. I remember how I looked forward to these chats; they were a breath of fresh air in my daily routine. Olivia was very smart and knew a lot about many subjects. She was never boring. Many times I shared my problems with her and she used to sit and listen attentively. She knew how much I liked to interact and meet new people.

One day she gave me a big blue envelope. "This is for you Itzik", she said quietly, as though she wanted to make sure that no one else would hear us. "I know how much you love people. I know you will enjoy it." She put the envelope on the table and left to get on with her work. Working in a bank, we had strict regulations. We were not allowed to receive gifts worth more than EUR 15 without filling in a form and declaring them. I was curious. I slowly opened the envelope and inside was an invitation for a reception and a private party hosted by the embassy of the African country Olivia had come from. The party was happening that weekend.

Wow! Interesting. How did this lady get hold of the invitation? I decided not to ask too many questions and go to the party.

It was an amazing event. I met a lot of people, including the local ambassador. We exchanged some ideas and opportunities and I mentioned that I'd got my invitation from Olivia, the lady at my office. The ambassador looked me directly in the eyes and said: "So you must be Isaac," (that's the name Olivia used to call me). My face went red with embarrassment. "Yes, true," I answered. He continued: "You look surprised. But do not worry, young man, Olivia said amazing things about you." I was confused, what could she have said about me? The ambassador smiled: "Olivia is my cousin."

During the following months my friendship with the ambassador developed. I won one of my biggest clients for the bank with his kind help; his country's largest oil and gas company. It all came from paying attention to another human being. Nobody could suspect that I talked to this lady so I could pitch to the oil and gas company. It was pure 'Attentional Networking'.

Attentional Networking is like a muscle: the more you practice it, the stronger it gets. The more you build it, the bigger it gets.

People tell me: 'You know everybody', or 'everybody knows you'. I must have been hearing this for the past 20 years. Why do they say that? What do they mean?

As long as I can remember, I've always approached new people every day and at every event I attend, I go on to develop this relationship, and to connect with and add value to those I meet. Some people see events with 5,000 participants or more as overwhelming, while I see them as a kind of Disneyland for relationship-building. You encounter many interesting people who you can start creating a relationship with (mostly business ones, but I also know some couples who met at these events and went on to get married).

Over the years I've become very well connected and a valuable resource for many people in my industry. Moreover, I became someone people can trust, and someone who would always listen to them. In today's world of information overload and economic fluctuations, a reputation defined by interest in other people and giving authentic attention is a good one to have. I became known as the 'Attentional Networker' (or as I prefer it an 'Authentic Attention relationship builder').

I really like to connect with people everywhere I go, on any occasion and at every opportunity. For me connecting with other people is a way of life, not a one-off event. Sometimes I feel it's like a drug for my soul: I am addicted to my interest in other people in a good way! If you observed any of my conversations, you would find clear evidence that I'm genuinely interested in other people. You'd see that I am authentic and that the attention to others comes from the heart. I like to ask questions and to listen to their stories. I find it interesting to learn about others; what is important to them, how they define success, what they need to become successful. This single skill continually brings me lucrative job opportunities and a very successful career. While other people were unable to find jobs and my competitors were struggling to find new clients, my personal marketability was growing and it continues expand. Do you know why? Because people value authenticity and being given attention.

I'm not writing this to impress you, but to share with you that everybody can do it and achieve amazing results. More importantly, YOU can do it with immediate effective and tangible results. Your time has come! So please stay with me. I'm happy to share all my secrets with you.

So how can you do it? How can you embrace and consistently practice 'Attentional Networking'?

'Attentional Networking' is for you

Every day you have opportunities to meet people. You can ignore them or you can practice your attentional networking skills. Using authentic attention is the key to connect with all these people, and if you utilize it properly, you will improve your life tremendously. I am sure that once you get more familiar with all the ingredients of attentional networking, your interaction with other people will never be the same again. So let's dive a bit deeper.

The idea behind giving attention and connecting with other people is to help, share, care and exchange ideas and information. Your attention to others is based on respect, trust, authenticity and integrity.

By interacting with others, with positive energy and enthusiasm, you learn more about their needs and desires. You'll create a genuine chemistry with others that will help you build a long-lasting relationship with them. So which part of this process do you have difficulty with? What prevents you from making it part of your daily routine? What could be negative about giving authentic attention to other people?

I don't blame you if you despise networking as it's almost become another name for selling and persuasion. Many who pride themselves on their networking skills are no more than business card collectors. Some of them are driven purely by self-interest. Online these people feel they're in a constant race to amass bigger numbers on social networks. They try to connect with everybody on LinkedIn or like every second post on Facebook or retweet anything others are tweeting without properly understanding what they're supporting or who they're giving attention to. They're the 'attention getters'. We call them 'the Network Jerks'. If you don't know how to properly connect and build a real life relationship, how can you do it online? No wonder many of these connections are artificial and devoid of any real value. I really feel sad for these people. You do not want to be like them.

Try being an 'Attentional Networker' instead. Be a sincere, authentic and nice human being. Feel genuine interest in other people. If you are a nice person, it'll be easy for you. But if you are an arrogant, selfish person without any interest in others, it will be very hard for you to become an attentional networker. Actually you're bound to fail. But I assume that you, my dear reader, do not belong to the latter group.

Attention and powerful human relations

A friend asked me: "How can I get rid of my preliminary judgment of other people, even before I've talked to them?" If your automatic preliminary review of another is negative, it will be very hard to give them pure authentic attention. Thus, no positive relationship can be developed. It's a good question and this is the right place to share my answer with you.

The thought you have about another person is your own. It belongs to you. The other person isn't responsible for that thought. Like every other thought, it's probably based on your past experiences and it comes unbidden from your subconscious mind.

What's the solution? Acknowledge your automatic thought and let it go. Start feeling and acting positively toward other people. By thinking well of others, you will think and attract good things to yourself.

The clear message I want you to get is: what you do to others, you do to yourself! So wish for others what you wish for yourself and give them your authentic attention. This is the first step to developing excellent interpersonal relationships.

Attentional Skill Set

"You must either modify your dreams or magnify your skills."

Jim Rohn

Toolkit for building sincere relationships

Building sincere relationships with other people is linked to the 'soft' skills. Connecting with people, giving them your attention, communicating (verbally or non-verbally), being a likeable personality, building trust and letting others believe in you and feel confidence with you are all part of the Attentional Networking toolkit.

If you are interested in advancing in life, you probably already participate in events and seminars and read a lot of books, articles and blogs about networking. So you may be asking what's new about Attentional Networking. You may even doubt the usefulness of investing time and energy in building relationships. So let me make it easier and clearer for you.

In most of the events you participated in or the books you have read, people discussed the concept of 'Networking' totally differently. They taught you how to get attention from other people, how to build relationships so it'll be easier to sell to these people at a later stage. They'll tell you that networking is soft selling. By building the relationship you are working to ensure that prospects will think about you when they are ready to buy. No wonder networking scares off a lot of people.

Thankfully 'Attentional Networking' demands a totally different set of skills – being a caring, thoughtful, empathic and sympathetic human being. It's all about giving attention to others rather than trying to get attention from them. It's a style of networking that brings amazing results in a much shorter time. Attentional Networking is a way of life. Once experienced, you will never let it go!

Did you ever wonder why people behave differently with their friends than they do with clients? Why should there be any difference? If you're an authentic person, you should be yourself all the time: online or offline, in public or in private, in a domestic environment or in a professional setting.

Our office was in a very tall building, a mini skyscraper. Companies like Google and Amazon also had their offices there. I remember getting in the elevator once and finding that I was the only man among twelve ladies. The doors closed and the elevator started ascending. I couldn't stay quiet a moment longer: "I hope this elevator gets stuck." All the ladies started laughing and we had a few seconds of joy. Afterwards, each time I met one of them they'd greet me with a big smile and we'd exchange a few more sentences. After three months of seeing me on almost a daily basis, one of them took the initiative and scheduled a meeting with me. We went on to realize an interesting business opportunity together. This is the power of being authentic all the time.

Over the years, I've often questioned why so many large clients decided to work with me. Why did I have this great network that stretched all around the world? Why was I always a few steps ahead of my competitors? How come I earned, even when I was an employee, three to four times more than colleagues who had the same knowledge, degrees and experience (and some even more than me)? Why was I chosen to join a company's board of directors that others were desperate to enter, with no success? Why, when I speak on stage or give my training, will people cry or hug me? I'm just a regular person. There's nothing special about me and my talents or skills.

After many years of searching, I found the answer.

So if you ask me what is the single important behaviour that you need to become a master in Attentional Networking, my answer will be short and simple – be a person who gives authentic attention.

Attentional listening

You don't want to miss out on any information shared with you. You won't know when and under which circumstances this information will be useful to you. So listen. Concentrate on the other person's needs and interests. If you listen carefully you will find opportunities, ideas, possibilities and a lot in common. I guarantee that if you start to listen carefully, you will find too many opportunities. Listening with your eyes and ears is much more powerful than talking with your mouth.

Are you familiar with the 'Kronman Principle' in Economics? Professor Kronman was the dean of Yale University and one of the areas he specialized in was contracts law. In his economic theory, he argues the distinction between deliberately acquired information and casually acquired information. Kronman gives a lot of emphasis on deliberately acquired information. How does this connect to our subject? When you are listening to somebody else, whether it's deliberate (i.e. a meeting) or not (for example you're listening to a conversation between two people on the train), you can learn a lot of valuable information (sometimes even ahead of the market). I want you to understand the power of information received by listening to another person.

What kind of reward do you get from listening to other people? First, by paying attention to another you benefit both parties, both the other person and yourself. Second, each person helps to enlarge your understanding and your life.

A few years ago, I went to visit a client of mine in Moscow. The account manager for this client, who was a native Russian speaker, also joined me. The only reason for the meeting was to receive a copy of the client's identity document and to identify him personally for compliance reasons.

We arrived early in the morning at a branch of one of the banks in Moscow and were shown into a waiting room. It was almost like a museum from Soviet times. You could smell the dust in the air, as if nobody had sat in there for centuries. After 30 minutes, a man asked us to follow him to another room on an upper floor where we would meet the client. The second room was larger than the first one and was decorated with antiques and old furniture. It looked like the place where the bank held its board meetings.

The door opened and a small muscular man dressed in a suit and a tie entered. His face was cold and he seemed in a rush. He addressed us in English with a heavy Russian accent: "Please sit down. What you want to drink? Black tea? Green tea? Water?" We sat down and my colleague started speaking in Russian. I was sitting to one side examining his body language and trying to understand his reply. I couldn't understand a single word. I was annoyed. I wanted to listen too. I felt there was much more to his man than just an ID card.

I decided to interfere and asked him which languages he spoke. He answered: "Russian, English and Hebrew." I felt like somebody had punched me in the face! He spoke Hebrew, my mother tongue! I was happy as a small child in a candy store and said: "Hebrew! Me too." "Really?" he asked and tried to impress me with a few words. He stood up, opened the closet behind him and brought out a bottle of vodka and two glasses. Next, he moved his chair to face me and started speaking to me. We were like two cousins who hadn't seen each other for a long time. He devoted all his attention to me.

My colleague was left out of the rest of the conversation. I whispered to her to let it go, since the client felt more comfortable now. We continued our chat (he spoke while I listened) for another 45 minutes. I learned that the client was also the chairman of the bank (that explains why we met in the boardroom) and owned another 24 companies. This was the beginning of a very successful friendship.

One of the most unappreciated attentional networking skills that you can easily master is the ability to listen. To get people excited about you and your business you need to do more listening and less talking. Good listening is active not passive.

How many times have you walked away from a conversation with someone and couldn't remember a word they'd said? You were there in body but not in mind. It's easy to 'zone out' and drift into your own thoughts, particularly if you are busy, bored, can't see the relevance or have made an assumption that there is nothing to gain from the discussion.

In an interesting blog titled: 'Key Networking Skills – Listening Skills' written by Opendoorz Professional Business Network, the concept of 'Engaged Attentional Listening' is discussed. Engaged Attentional Listening is when you understand a conversation and could answer someone else's questions about what they've said. Fully engaged listening takes this to the highest level. You not only hear and understand what has been said but you have a sense of who the person is, what their passions and experiences are, and what really makes them tick.

One of the most profound points Dale Carnegie made in his book 'How to Win Friends and Influence People' was that people love to talk about themselves. If you can get people to discuss their experiences and opinions—while listening with sincere interest and giving real attention—you can have a great conversation with someone without having to say much at all.

Attentional Networking Listening Skills Tip:

A good listener actively pays authentic attention to the conversation and responds appropriately with questions.

The power of a smile

A friend of mine is extraordinarily successful. Another acquaintance of mine was writing an article and wanted me, as a good networker, to introduce her to my friend so she could interview him. As promised, I arranged a dinner which they both attended. During our dinner the lady asked my friend to share the secret of his success. My friend looked at me, with a beaming smile, and then with his big captivating smile, just looked at the lady. She immediately responded: "I get it...WOW! I even feel it!" What did she mean? This was part of my friend's personality. His natural charm, kindness and likeability where all expressed perfectly in his smile. It seems that nobody could resist his smile, since it was a pure act of authentic attention. How many people give you this feeling when you meet them?

I can think of at least of one example of a human being who is always happy to see us. Did you guess who? A baby. A baby's smile could melt the hearts of the saddest people in the universe.

A smile is a ticket to a person's heart. Smiling is a simple attention-giving tool. It is basic behaviour, yet people just don't think about doing it. People are more likely to warm up to someone with a broad smile on his face than they are to someone with a dour countenance.

The power of a smile comes across even in a telephone conversation. Try it for yourself. Say the same sentence once as normal and then repeat it while smiling. Listen to the change in your voice.

Smiles go a long way. Ron Gutman reviewed studies about smiling and found that a smile can predict how long you will live. He discovered that a simple smile has a measurable effect on your overall well-being. British researchers have found that one smile can provide the same level of brain stimulation as up to 2,000 chocolate bars. Smiling is also contagious, especially when you combine it with sincere attention. In Stanley Gordon West's 'Growing an Inch', he famously wrote, "Smile and the world smiles with you, cry and you cry alone."

A smile conveys a message of joy and a willingness to build a relationship with the other person. You must have a good time meeting and being with other people if you want them to feel the same about you.

Do you know the meaning of my name? The anglicized version is Isaac and is a transliteration of the Hebrew term which literally means "he laughs/will laugh". So laughing and smiling is inherent in my name. I try to live up to it every day. I smile at my family in the morning, I smile at my neighbours, I smile at the reception lady in our building, I smile at my colleagues, I smile at strangers in line at lunch. What do you think happens? Everybody smiles back at me.

Sometimes, people ask me what is wrong with me or why I'm so happy. I even got a message from a person I've known since elementary school asking me if something was wrong, why was I so happy? Am I really so odd? Judge for yourself. The fact is that my smile helps me listen to people and give them my sincere attention more easily. They know it, they feel it, they want it and it brings me a lot of great results.

If you want to give authentic attention to others, be happy, smile. Work on your thoughts and direct them on to happy, positive subjects. I find listening to one of my favourite songs with the volume turned high helps me get into a great mood. How will you direct your mindset toward happiness? How will you condition your thoughts and reprogram your inner you? Remember, it is your thoughts that control your ability to be happy. You will be happy as much as you make up your mind to be.

On one my first business trips to India I ended one of my meetings earlier than expected. So I went out to the main road to wait for my driver. While waiting, I saw two small skinny children walking along laughing. I followed them with my eyes until they entered a small tent at the corner of the street. I decided to go and check it out. I gently stuck my head inside and saw a photo of an old lady. A few seconds later, I was approached by a smiling young lady, who invited me to enter. "Come in, come in... Do you want a drink?" I politely refused. She explained that this small tent had been the family home for the past 40 years and the photo was of her mother who had passed away a few years before. There were six people living on this small corner of the street. My head started spinning with thoughts. I realized for the first time in my life that happiness and smiling have nothing to do with what you have or who you are. These people had nothing, but their minds were happy.

Perhaps this is why Mother Teresa said:

> ## "I will never understand all the good that a simple smile can accomplish."

You know now how true it is, but only if your smile is authentic and warm!

The name of the person is the sweetest sound he has ever heard

"What do you want to drink sir?" She asked.
"Coke zero agent 007."

She was surprised, but understood after a few seconds and started laughing.

"You know, now that I think about it, you are so right!"

I was in the middle of a flight from Amsterdam to New York with KLM, the Dutch Royal airlines. You probably noticed that airlines make sure each employee has a name badge. That was the case for years. Until recently when KLM decided to change the name badge for one that only carried the title of the employee, such as junior agent or senior agent.

So even if you wanted to talk to the stewardess, you couldn't address them by their name anymore. KLM had done it after it was found that illegal immigrants had been using fake security badges (some of them were KLM badges) at an airport in the US. The immigrants had been arrested.

I think the company over-reacted. Taking the name from the badge doesn't help to create closer client relationships either! I even wrote a letter to the CEO of KLM (which was never answered) and advised him to give each employee a 'fake' name to be used only at work, exactly as artists have. So on the one hand nobody would arrest these employees and on the other hand travelers could address the employee in their 'work' name.

Why is a name so important? Dale Carnegie said:

> "Remember that a person's name is to that person the sweetest and the most important sound in any language."

I wanted to show a group of people how this basic element can create magic. It was the night before I was supposed to give my attentional networking workshop to this group in London. We all went out for dinner. Since we were a big group, we were separated over a few tables with five or six people at each one. A few minutes passed and a waitress with curly blonde hair and a blank face gave us some menus. She'd seen the size of our group and knew she'd have to work hard. While she was giving us the menus and asking for our drinks order, I noticed her name badge.

Her name was Ewa (Eva). I took a guess that she was Polish. My turn came and she asked me: "What can I get you mister?"
"Still water and a big smile, dziekuje." (This means thank you in Polish and is pronounced 'jen-ku-je').
Her blue eyes shone as she smiled. "How do you know I am Polish!?"
All the people on our table started laughing and smiling back at her.

We got amazing service, every time she came to us she lit up with a bright smile.

Later that evening, I found out from Ewa's colleagues that it was her birthday the following day. We surprised her just before leaving the restaurant by singing 'Happy Birthday'. All the guests in the restaurant spontaneously joined in. It was an amazing atmosphere. I'm sure nobody in the group will ever forget that evening. Much more than that, Ewa will never forget it. This is how magical a name can be.

Every person is interested in their own name and they'll snap to attention as soon as they hear it. Imagine you're at a cocktail party surrounded by noise and chatter. Now imagine that someone calls your name. Do you pay attention? Even if you're in the middle of an interesting conversation you will still hear your name (even if it's only subconsciously).

But it also works in the opposite direction. I get very irritated when somebody misspells my name when replying to an email from me. My name is Itzik, but sometimes people write ItziEk (ziek means sick in Dutch). How can they make this mistake? Didn't they see how I signed my own email? They could easily have copied and pasted my name! Over the years, I've come to think that people who misspell my name in an email won't pay sincere attention in real life (you do not have to agree with me on that one). So many times, I've skipped building relationships with these people.

How do you remember people's names? Sometimes it is difficult, even for me, to remember a person's name or even how to pronounce it. Some people have nicknames to remember too. Chinese business people also have a traditional Western name (often it's included on their business cards). In most cases, this name has nothing to do with their real Chinese name. So why is that? The Chinese understand the importance of a name, and also how essential it is to put the other person at ease. So to make our life comfortable they adopt an English name, so we can address them easily. Isn't that considerate?

Let me give you two techniques that will help you remember people's names. First, ask the person to repeat their name several times and even to spell it out for you. It gives the opposite impression than you'd think. It really shows that you are interested in their name. Even if you forget it the next time you see the person, there's nothing wrong with asking them to remind you of it.

The second technique is borrowed from a book on how to boost your memory. Let's do a short exercise to illustrate how it works. Imagine I'm going to give you a list of one hundred pairs of words and ask you to remember them: pink house, white elephant and so on. Now, imagine a surreal picture next to each pair of words. With white elephant, you could see yourself holding a bottle of Tipp-Ex (the white correction liquid) and painting an elephant with it. Do you see the picture vividly in your mind? If I ask you a year from now what the colour of the elephant was, you will still remember that it was white. Sometimes I hold the other person's business card in the air next to their face and take a virtual photo of them with their card. I trained my mind to store these images so every time I see them, I'll see their business card and their name right beside their face.

Learning the name of the person is an important part of paying attention and building relationships so you need to invest the necessary time and energy in remembering it. Nobody will accept any excuses from you. By using a person's name, you will let them know that you are really interested in building a relationship with them. It is simple, yet how many people do it on a daily basis?

I've participated in many conferences in my life. I've met a lot of people and made a lot of introductions. Strangers often spend a few minutes in conversation and move on without learning each other's names. How stupid is that?

I believe that if you care about a person and sincerely want to build a relationship with them you must learn their name and use it as often as you can. Can you imagine a relationship between a husband and wife who don't remember each other's name? So how can you dare to build a business partnership if you don't know the other person's name? I rest my case.

Follow up with your personal attention

Those who are interested in getting attention from others want to be remembered, but as an Attentional Networker, you are interested in remembering other people. Remembering other people includes remembering their names, their needs, how you can help them, what they like and what they dislike. Nowadays, we need to store a lot of information so we can use it in the future.

The process of building a relationship does not end when your meeting does. The meeting is just the beginning. It's very important that you follow up consistently. You need to make the extra effort if you want these people to establish a relationship with you.

Many years ago I was invited to dinner at a friend's house. He'd invited 60 people to celebrate the start up of his new company. Among the friends and family were some people he wanted to build stronger relationships with. Before the dinner started, my friend took me to one side. He knew that my expertise was in developing relationships with other people. He showed me an old business card. "This card is from Albert, the guy sitting over there at the table with his wife. I met him a few years ago and I followed your advice about writing down specific information about him on the back of his business card."

He turned the card over: "Do you see here? You can still read what I wrote: 'eats only fish'. So we cooked fish especially for Albert and his wife... That's good, right?" It was as though he was waiting for my approval. I gave him a slap on the back and we returned to the table to join the other guests. At the end of the dinner, we noticed that Albert and his wife had not eaten their food. It was quite embarrassing. It turned out that since my friend had met Albert, he'd got married and he and his wife had become strict vegetarians. My friend forgot one of the basic rules of Attentional Networking – follow up regularly.

Simple attentive follow up will differentiate you from 99% of the population. Most people follow up only when they need something from the other person. Unfortunately, you rarely meet people who follow up just because they are interested in you. Isn't it true that you always follow up with the people you care about – your family, your friends –on a regular basis? So why not follow up in the same way with every person you meet and want to develop a relationship with?

Many people see the holiday season as a good opportunity to follow up. But is that true? I don't think people really care about Christmas cards. To prove my point, I decided one year not to send any cards to my contacts. After the holiday season was over, I invited three colleagues into my room and called a few of the clients. I asked each of them how they'd liked my card and they all said they'd liked it very much. Strange considering that I hadn't sent any that year. If you really want to follow up, if you really want others to see that you care about them and you think about them, send them a card on a normal day. No special reason; just wish them a nice day. Maybe they will think you're weird, but they will never forget you!

You may choose to follow up in any way you think. You can send an email and remind the other person where you met and remind them of your conversation. It is very important to make it personal, to make it YOUR follow up.

As an international tax lawyer I often participated in conferences or other events around the world. Many times when I got back to my office I'd get several 'mass-destruction' emails. I refer to those people who dump all the business cards they collected at the event on their secretary and ask them to send a 'follow up' email to everyone. They're the sort of emails that start with words like: 'It was nice meeting you at..." and lead straight into a hard sell of their company's products and services. The email shows no interest in you, they have no clue who you are, and there's no personal message.

The emails went straight into my trash. These people weren't interested in me. What makes me sad is the fact that they think they did the follow up, that thing they'd learned in the last 'Networking' workshop they attended. Sometimes when I had to cancel my participation at the last moment and my name remained on the list of participants, I'd still get these sad 'follow up' emails! Guess how these emails start? "It was nice meeting you..."

Always continue to give your authentic attention to other people in your follow up actions. Focus on how you can help them, how you can support their needs, how you can add value to them.

A handwritten note works brilliantly. How many people still write notes? You could attach this note to an interesting article or some other information that the other person would be interested in reading. The idea is to continue your real interest in and attention to the other person, even when you aren't physically nearby. Don't let 'out of sight, out of mind' be your reality.

When I send a follow up email, I always write very specific and even emotional messages. I may write: "It was amazing meeting you; your positive energies brightened my day." In the past, I thought I shouldn't write like that or people would think I was an oddball, especially in business. But over the years, I learned to trust my connecting skills. I want the other person to feel the warmth I have for them, almost as though the email can give them a big warm hug.

To my surprise, not only do people accept it, their replies are just as heart-warming. You should definitely try this exercise yourself; you will be amazed at the results. Let your follow up action clearly reflect who you are!

Attentional Mindset

"As you think so shall you be!
Since you cannot physically
experience another person,
you can only experience them in your mind.
Conclusion: all of the other people in your life
are simply thoughts in your mind.
Not physical beings to you, but thoughts.
Your relationships are all in how
you think about the other people of your life.
Your experience of all those people
is only in your mind.
Your feelings about your lovers
come from your thoughts.
For example, they may in fact behave
in ways that you find offensive.
However, your relationship to them
when they behave offensively is not
determined by their behavior,
it is determined only by how you choose
to relate to that behavior.
Their actions are theirs,
you cannot own them,
you cannot be them,
you can only process them in your mind."

Dr Wayne Dyer

Your attention attitude

How important is your attitude? Any relationship specialist will tell you that your attitude is everything. Its important then that you pay attention to your attitude and make sure it's set to 'positive'. Every time you meet someone you should be able to give them your authentic attention, even if it is in the middle of the night at the airport.

I was tired out and heading for home after a few hectic days of meetings and training engagements. My flight was due to leave 1am. I was half asleep as I waited to check in. Out of the corner of my eye I watched an older couple trying to check in. I noticed that the man could barely walk. Without thinking, I opened the security rope and invited them to go ahead of me in the line. Why did I do it? Well, I noticed that the man was a famous businessman and I wanted to offer him my services... I'm joking! I did it because my attitude is ready all the time, even late at night. By the way, a month later the gentleman asked for my help in expanding his company's services to a few other countries. I happily agreed. He turned out to own one of the largest IT companies in Europe.

It's not always easy to give your attention to others, meet new people, and keep in touch with them.

How many times have you sent emails or called somebody simply to follow up and the other person did not reply or return your call? Did you give up? Did you speculate, like I mistakenly used to, that the other person was not interested in you? I even used to send emails asking the other person (quite stupidly) if the reason they hadn't answered was because I'd insulted them! This didn't do anything for my attitude. My advice to you is to keep trying and keep your attitude set to 'positive'. You're still interested in building a strong relationship with them, so don't give up! Practice this expression we have in the Netherlands: 'Nee heb je, ja kan je krijgen' which means: 'No – you have already. Yes – you can get'. In other words, you already have a non-relationship with the other person; this is your status quo. But if you build a relationship with them you'll get something good if you maintain the right attitude.

On one occasion, I desperately wanted to have a meeting with somebody, but did not get a reply. So I decided to take action. I found out that she used to buy a coffee from the Starbucks across from her office every morning. I went there the next day and asked to speak with the shift manager. I handed him a nice card and asked him to hand it to the lady I wanted to talk to when he gave her the coffee. It was a done deal. She arrived and placed her order a few minutes later. I signaled to the manager, as we'd agreed, that this was the right lady. The moment I was waiting for arrived. She received her coffee as well as a card, which was tied to the coffee cup with a nice ribbon. I could see that she was very surprised and happy. She invited me to her office right away so we could have a short coffee break together. It was a great meeting and we're still friends today (right, Miss G?) But more surprising for me was to find out that she'd never received any of my emails; her personal assistant had lost her job the week before and forgot to mention my calls. Do you see how maintaining a great authentic attitude all the time will win you opportunities to connect with amazing people?

As an effective authentic relationship-builder, you'll need to have a consistent caring attitude about other people.

Share or die

The more you share, the less lonely you will be.

In order to understand yourself, your limits, abilities, and things you need to improve on when giving attention to others; you'll constantly need to work on yourself. Meeting people will help you practice your attentional networking skills. You need to work hard at staying in touch and being visible. You need to continue to be attentive to your family, friends and acquaintances. The other option is to become lonely, something I do not wish for you my friend!

It helps to see the act of sharing your attention with others as a fun activity – as a joyful way to live your life and give to others. The more great people you meet, the more chances you'll have to meet even more great people.

Sharing increases your chances of developing sincere relationships with the right people for you.

I was always bothered by one basic flaw in the way legal firms operated. Many partners would try to 'score' – they'd try to commandeer every new prospect that joined the firm. Thus, they'd get paid for every bit of business that came from the client. I won't confuse you with the different mechanisms developed by the firms to make this system work fairly as that's not relevant here. The point I am trying to make is that they've got it wrong.

Imagine you are a partner in a law firm and you are responsible for the labour law department. You get a new client. If the client is dissatisfied with your services, he will leave the firm. Now, assume that after welcoming this client to your department, you introduce him to your other partners. That way the client may use a few of your firm's services. The client will develop a relationship with a few of the partners, not just you. Wouldn't it be harder for the client to leave now that he has a working relationship with several of the partners? So sharing your contacts will actually help you build better, stronger and longer-lasting relationships. It's the antithesis to the way professional firms operate. I think it is time for them to wake up and learn the art of attentional networking.

The beauty of attentional networking is that you have to spread your caring more widely in order to become successful. The more you keep the attention only to yourself, the more selfish you become. The more selfish you become, the more likely your destiny will be to die alone, with no friends, no real relationships, nobody to care for you. Sad!

How can you use sharing to enhance your relationship skills? Next time you're due to meet a stranger, invite somebody you already know to the meeting (it could be your assistant or trainee) who may also learn from meeting this new person. Sharing will benefit you instantly. You will make sure this new person gets attention not only from you, but from another person. Assuming that the attention is warm and authentic, it will help build a stronger relationship for all parties.

While writing these lines, I've just thought of another benefit – you will be obliged in this meeting to give attention to both your old contact and the new contact. Thus, you will continue to strengthen your relationship with your existing contact.

Please remember that it is not just about sharing, it is about sharing with the right people. You need to make sure that the people who'll join your meeting or will share your new contact are the right ones. You'll develop a good instinct for this over time. At the beginning though, choose carefully as it is your name that's on the line.

When attentional networking becomes part of your personality, you will sometimes be joined by others when you are meeting a new party. Please refuse any 'forced' sharing. These incidents are not helpful – they can actually be harmful to the new relationship you are trying to forge. Such situations have occasionally happened to me during events and conferences. While you want to fully focus your attention on what this new person is sharing with you, suddenly, out of nowhere, comes this ex-colleague or a person pretending to be your best friend. A few seconds after greeting you, they jump on the other person and force them to engage in a conversation. It's a bit like an eagle going in for the kill. I really dislike this sort of behaviour. Mainly because if your new contact really thinks this other person is your friend, it could harm your own relationship and authenticity. Remember, I warned you!

It is interesting to note that people, in general, feel comfortable with sharing and growing their network online. It just proves to you that it works.

What happens when you share your contacts or share your attention with more people? Two very magical things: you build trust with other people in your network, and from there you build empathy. Note that I'm not talking about sympathy. Sympathy is when you feel badly for someone who's had something bad happen to them. Empathy is when you actually share the emotions of others. It's a powerful and deeply primal experience.

Be passionate

What about sharing your passions with others?

First let's discover how passionate you are. Ask yourself the following questions:

- Are you really passionate about meeting other people?
- Or are you doing it because you have to?
- When you are with others, do you feel excited?

Passion helps you fall in love with life and enjoy the things you are doing. Do yourself a favour, from tomorrow and each day that follows drop just one activity that you are not passionate about. This will make room for new inspirations and possibilities to enter your life.

What does passion have to do with giving your attention to other people and building relationships? Passion (from the Latin verb patī meaning to suffer) is now applied to every powerful feeling, not only the negative ones. Passion means an intense emotion or strong desire for something. For years, I struggled to understand how people could build relationships with others unless they had a strong desire to do so. Isn't it obvious that your basic network always starts in the areas you are passionate about? With limited time and a priceless attention resource, isn't it time to pay special attention to the activities you enjoy the most and those you most want to connect with?

These days passion also brings people together online through social networks. I'm sure you're aware of it and how contagious it is.

If you want to authentically connect with others, you want them to truly know who you are, what you like, and what you care about. Passion is the tool that attracts and draws other people to you, be it in business or personal life.

I've shared many times on stage my belief that 'people bond when they are having fun'. When do you really get to know people: when you sit next to them in a seminar or when you go out to have dinner or a drink together? Do you agree that passion and a great atmosphere create an open environment and a feeling of comfort that helps people bond? Your passion is like superglue – it holds people together. It will create a deeper bonding with others, especially those you are interested in building a relationship with. Passion helps you pay special attention to the people you are most comfortable with and to the activities you most enjoy.

My growing interest in other people, along with my successful track record in helping companies expand and grow internationally, is the main reason I founded my group. My group focuses on growth strategies, relationship capital and training for enhancing business and personal relationships. That might mean creating a structure for a corporate international expansion or designing a business development and networking training and strategy to help a company expand. We also build and facilitate a client relationship program that helps participants acquire new relationships and maintain existing ones. I trust it is not a surprise for you, dear friend, that I see Attentional Networking as an effective way to build and maintain relationships, be they business or personal.

Passion makes you different. To me, being passionate means differentiating yourself from others when it comes to building relationships. I believe that your positive energies and passion show other people that you are someone worth talking to. People would be happy to spend time with you and enjoy your attention. Moreover, you will become someone worth talking about!

Be interested and interesting

Being a person who gives attention to others isn't just about being a good communicator, you need to be interesting and interested in others at the same time. What do I mean?

Your special expertise, your knowledge and abilities, all make you unique and inspire others' interest in you. This is the only way to attract the right people to become part of your own network.

Do you get my point? Start believing that in every step of your career, you gain new expertise and new knowledge that makes you different from other people. Thus, every person has their own unique attention giving skills. Your uniqueness makes you more valuable when building relationships with other people. This inimitable content and knowledge create your own 'fingerprints' in your interaction with others.

Starting from today, you need to inventory the exceptional knowledge, skills and expertise that you already have or still need to acquire. They will provide real value to others and support you in giving them your sincere attention.

Here are some tips and ideas on how to develop your interest in others and become a better attention giver:

1.   Know to ask

Everybody can ask questions, but asking interesting and original questions is a key differentiator in your relationship with others. Develop your own style of asking questions and you will show your real interest in others.

2.   Learn, learn, learn

Great attention-givers are constantly looking out for new knowledge. You need to learn and develop yourself all the time. This can be done in many ways, for instance by reading books, or attending seminars or webinars. Knowledge will give you the confidence to develop relationships with others, to hold an interesting conversation, and pay the other person your attention.

3.　Broaden your horizons

You need to experience more in life. Be curious about people outside your industry and beyond your comfort zone. Broaden your horizons. Learn new skills, even if they have nothing to do with your profession. Unusual experiences will make you a more interesting person as well as opening your own mind.

4.　Build your strengths

Many people try to correct and work on their weaknesses, while taking their strengths for granted. Isn't it easier to become better and more focused on your strengths, so your weaknesses won't be noticed? Building your strengths will get others interested in you and your experiences.

5.　Keep going

How many times have you tried to reach another person and they didn't return your email or call? I used to get discouraged when it happened to me and start speculating that they didn't like me. Don't make the same mistake! Keep going. Being unique, being different and authentic can sometimes scare other people. They don't dare to be like you (even though many of them wished they could!) Keep going and try to connect with others with authenticity and sincerity. Keep your eyes and heart on the results. Let them surprise you and encourage you to take more actions.

6.　Tell inspiring stories

Good storytelling is a skill. Telling compelling stories with powerful content is an art. Telling an inspiring story not only grabs the other person's attention and interest, it can also energize your network to help you achieve your goals and aspirations. Simple and universal stories will stoke your passion and make you interesting to others. Words are part of 'paying attention' – choose the right words, pay better attention and tell a Superior Story. Real stories ignite emotion within the other person. It's powerful, so use it in the right way!

Attention breeds loyalty

Do you know the difference between satisfied and loyal? In your business relationships are your customers satisfied with your services or are they loyal? Are you satisfied or loyal to your spouse?

Many people mistake customer satisfaction and customer loyalty and assume that they're essentially the same thing. Actually, they're quite different. Satisfaction relates to the results of a process, whether it's the sales process, service, or product performance. Loyalty, on the other hand, is a much longer-term proposition. Loyalty relates to a relationship—one that can actually survive a negative product or service process.

Authentic attention breeds loyalty. Truly loyal connections look beyond the occasional negative experiences and continue building a relationship with us for the long run. Satisfied connections do not necessarily become loyal relationships. Thus, when you give your authentic attention to another human being, you truly expect to create a relationship based on loyalty. So it's no wonder that you get hurt if this person betrays your trust!

Expect the unexpected

> "To expect the unexpected shows
> a thoroughly modern intellect."
>
> Oscar Wilde

How many times have you gained a new business relationship because you did something unusual or even unexpected? How many times did you give an authentic attention to another human being in an unexpected way or in unexpected circumstances? I always believe that giving authentic attention in unusual ways or at unexpected times can create greater results than doing it in the usual way.

I was introduced by a good friend to a very interesting and promising medical company. My international business structuring and tax knowledge was requested. A meeting was arranged. I felt very positive when I entered the boardroom. It was one of those days when you feel really great and the energy is flowing through your body. Soon after, we were joined by a very intelligent lady, the CFO of the company, and two other ladies from the legal department. It felt great; I was surrounded by four ladies, almost like being back at home with my four sisters. Then a tall man with thick white hair joined us. He was the CEO. He introduced himself with a big smile and the meeting started. Fifteen minutes into the meeting and it was my turn to explain and share my ideas with the others. I dived straight into the details.

Then, out of nowhere, I looked at the CEO and told him: "Do you know you have sex appeal?" There was silence in the room. Everybody looked at me as if they were wondering if they'd really heard me right. Then the CEO stood up, opened his arms and said to me: "Come here and give me a hug." He looked at my friend and said: "I don't know where you got this man, but I want only him. Do you hear me? I want only him." Everybody laughed and the CEO gave me a big bear hug. It was an awesome feeling. Why? Because I'd taken a risk and been myself. My friend asked me afterwards where I'd got this mad idea from and I really didn't have any convincing explanation. I only knew it felt good.

It feels good when you are open, authentic and transparent. It's the only way you can create a real relationship that gives you results. That company became a large client of mine. I am still in personal contact with the CEO and we meet up every now and then.

Did I expect anything when I said what I said? Absolutely not! The unexpected situation, the special (and maybe strange) circumstances attracted the other person to me. All the people in the meeting, including myself, knew that I had given an authentic attention to the CEO and that instantly got his commitment and interest.

Unexpected situations like that exist in anybody's life. Learn to recognize them and turn them into real powerful moments to bond and give authentic attention to other people. I promise you, you will never regret it!

21+1 Unique Tips
for Attentional Networking
that actually work

"Some of the biggest challenges
in relationships come from
the fact that most people
enter a relationship
in order to get something:
they're trying to
find someone
who's going to make
them feel good.
In reality, the only way
a relationship will last
is if you see your relationship
as a place that you go to give,
and not a place that you go to take."

Anthony Robbins

After reading this chapter, do you believe, as I do, that networking and creating relationships should be authentic, simple and sincere? So why are so many people uncomfortable with networking? Did you know that if you add the special ingredient called ATTENTION you will instantly become a successful networker and be able to build long-lasting relationships with your clients?

I have no doubt that you give sincere and friendly attention to people you know. However, because many of us (mistakenly) see networking as a 'business activity' it's easy to think that we need to act in a different way. Unfortunately, searching on the internet or participating in networking events, gives us the feeling that most networking strategies are pushy, needy, or self-serving — even though the people using them rarely act that way in day-to-day life. We rarely get real attention from the people we interact with at these events.

So what can we do? There are genuine ways to pay attention to others and help everyone become a better networker and relationship-builder. Here are some ideas that definitely work for me, helping me to create authentic, sincere relationships by using the power of Attentional Networking.

Attentional networking – what do you want to achieve?

1.   **Attentional Networking = the art of helping others.** Do you like to help other people? Do you do it genuinely without expecting them to help you in return? Focus on giving value to others without asking for help from them. Surprise others, especially when they don't expect to get your help. Provide them with great value added ideas, services and so on.

2.   **Attentional Networking = the art of servicing others' needs.** The first rule of building and developing a relationship with someone is to give them your complete attention by thinking about them. It is useless just adding people to your list of contacts without understanding who they are, what their needs are, what they want to achieve and how you can support them to achieve it faster and better. You need to give your attention to each detail, no shortcuts.

Attentional Networking
– how do you set your expectations?

3.   **Attentional Networking = The art of knowing the right people.** In the networking world, we name the person who goes around and hands out business cards to everyone 'the network jerk'. You should avoid being one of them! Isn't it more fun and joyful to only include in your network people you really care about? I have a surprise for you – there are enough good and nice people in every industry. Get them to be part of your network and give them and only them your undivided and sincere attention.

4.   **Attentional Networking = The art of giving with no limits.** When you sincerely do somebody a favour, do you expect to get something back from them? If you have ever given a positive answer to this question, then there is something wrong. How can you be sincere and at the same time expect to get a favour in return? Isn't it up to the other person? Paying attention to others means learning more about them, finding out why they are so interesting, being curious about them and how you can help them. Don't spoil it by expecting anything in return.

5.   **Attentional Networking = The art of focusing your attention on specific people.** Some blogs and articles say that networking is normal behaviour and there's no need to plan it. I partially agree, though I believe that if you want to use 'Attentional Networking' you should be strict with yourself in deciding and defining what you are looking for within your network. Please don't get me wrong, networking is also fun and you'll accidentally stumble across someone amazing once in a while. Even then you'll need to use sincere attention to build this relationship. Be proactive and create a list of people who you want to contact and who deserve your attention.

6.   **Attentional Networking = The art of going beyond your circle.** Did you ever participate in an event for a totally different industry? It happened to me, several times...by mistake...but I enjoyed it a lot. Meeting people outside your industry may be scary to a lot of people, but it is a

fulfilling experience. You learn to practice giving your sincere attention to other people. Since you are not from the same industry, you have no fear about connecting with the leading and most senior people there (as you probably don't who they are). You only need to give them your full attention by listening to them. It's easy! You'll be the person with a broad network, who can connect people across industries.

7.   **Attentional Networking = The art of noticing with empathy the existence of other people in your life.** How much do you try to measure in advance if people are relevant to you and your goals before trying to approach them? Giving attention to another human being should be a random, open and supportive act. Try to avoid those tools that are supposed to help you find the relevant people to network with. If you divide people into 'relevant' and 'irrelevant' you're not a real networker and you're getting in the way of what networking is really about – the ability to give attention to other people whoever they are.

Attentional Networking – how do you connect with new people?

8.   **Attentional Networking = The art of noticing other people's needs (rather than your own needs).** Creating new relationships doesn't come easily to everyone (maybe you are one of these people). Some people think in terms of time and money. So when you approach you can almost see them thinking 'how long will it take me? Can I earn anything by making contact with this person?' People are busy, so you need to use your attention to address those concerns at the start. Just ask if they have time to talk right now. Asking questions like this shows your sincere interest in the other person and your attention to their needs and limited resources. These sorts of questions may even shift the attention to you, as you are already demonstrating that you are both sincere and professional.

9.   **Attentional Networking = The art of offering praise, rather than requesting help.** The first time you give attention to someone is a special occasion. Don't mess it up by asking for anything from them! Attention is

the ability to give a sincere compliment to another human being. This act is so powerful that it can be kept short.

Don't destroy the purity of this genuine attention by asking for a favour, advice, or a promotion! Give the other person time to accept your praise, so laying the foundation for building your future relationship.

10.   **Attentional Networking = The art of being friendly and concise.** Can you start a relationship based on sincere attention via email? Yes! If your first contact is by email, then my best advice is to keep it short, sincere and friendly. You can dedicate this first interaction to complimenting the other person. Trust me, but you do not even need to explain at length why you are contacting them. This is attention, undivided, focused, authentic and brief. It will resonate in the other person's mind for a long time and it will definitely make you stand out from other correspondents.

11.   **Attentional Networking = The art of increasing the 'YES' attitude.** I was recently talking to a CEO of a multinational about offering a new training for his board of directors and senior management (how to win new clients by using unique attentional communication strategies). I started by asking for permission to continue and asked if he would like to know more. He was interested and we ended up having a great conversation.

There are some situations where you need to ask for something, but don't have the time to build a relationship and get to know the other party. This is the special magic of attention. The ability to weave in requests before you make an offer gets sincere attention from the other person. Thus, the odds of your offer being accepted will drastically increase. This specific act (as we call it – permission attention) can work wonders.

Attentional networking – how do you really create sincere relationships?

12.   **Attentional Networking = the art of providing real value to others.** The more value you create, the more it will come back to you

many times over. Focus all of your networking efforts and give your real attention to helping the people you contact.

13.   **Attentional Networking = the art of being friendly and supportive.** How hard is it to be friendly? This is a simple way of showing your real interest in others and building an authentic network. You should be supportive and friendly with others in every interaction you have with them. Moreover, find new and creative ways to be friendly. Have you read an article that someone in your network would enjoy? Tell them about it or send them a copy. Are you using something that would help a friend with a project they're working on? Send it to them. Have you met somebody interesting who may help someone you already know? Introduce the two of them. I'm sure you'll enjoy giving to others.

14.   **Attentional Networking = the art of sharing contacts and information**. Do you want know an easy and powerful way to enhance your network? Try to connect like-minded people from your existing network with each other and watch what happens. This idea seems foreign to many people, but it is actually quite easy. Do you know two people who follow the same sports team? Or have the same hobby? Or work in the same industry? Or live in the same area? I trust you understand the point I am trying to make. The more you pay attention to people and their individual backgrounds the better you can be in this match-making process. Simply introduce the two of them to each other. They can decide if they want to pursue the relationship further. Trust me, even if they aren't interested, they will appreciate the offer.

15.   **Attentional Networking = the art of nurturing your current network.** Are you aware that your friends and co-workers are part of your current network? Using Attentional Networking to build your relationships, start by giving sincere attention to your existing contacts. You don't need to wait to get new contacts before practicing real attentional networking.

Attentional Networking – how do you make networking a habit?

16.   **Attentional Networking = The art of attention to one person that leads to connection with many people.** Significant networks can only grow if you give real attention to real people. If you give sincere attention to only one person a day, your network will grow by at least with five more people a week (assuming that you do not network over the weekend). From my own experience, sincere attention to one person leads to connection with far more people than you would expect. Thus, you're bound to make significant progress.

17.   **Attentional Networking = The art of choosing the right time to connect**. A successful connection partly depends on your timing, the circumstances, if the other person is having a good or bad day and so on. So my suggestion to you is to do your best to choose the right time to share the attention that the other person deserves. It may be that all you get is a straightforward "No". If so, don't take it to heart. In most cases, it's not a reflection on you or what you said.

18.   **Attentional Networking = The art of follow up with attention**. The quality of your network depends on the quality of your follow up actions. To maintain good relations and pay real attention to other people's needs, you need to follow up, follow up, follow up in a very structured way. Be persistent! Following up with relevant conversation helps to anchor your previous interaction in their mind and displays more personality than just sending a bland "thanks for meeting up!"message.

Attentional Networking – important things to remember

19.   **Attentional Networking = The art of attention and intention to help other people, rather than yourself.** If you engage with others in a helpful way, if you give them real attention because they deserve it, you will build trust. Moreover, there is a good chance that they will like you ('the L factor'). People enjoy doing business with those they trust and like. Offering sincere attention and real help to other people will surely support your growing relationship with them.

20.   **Attentional Networking = The art of listening to what others have to say.** Take the time to listen to people's stories. This is giving real attention to the information they are sharing with you. You can only provide something of value to them if you listen to who they are and what they do.

21.   **Attentional Networking = The art of building relationships in the most unexpected places.** Have you ever volunteered for an event which was attended by particularly interesting participants or assistants? These places offer you a great opportunity to develop new relationships. Working on a project with a stranger is one of the best ways to develop a sincere relationship with them (and some of them can be very influential people!)

21+1. Attentional Networking = The art of letting others hear your voice!

Do you want to achieve real results? Do you want to show another person that you are paying attention to them? Then don't be afraid to pick up the phone, propose a video chat, or arrange a face-to-face meeting. Email is quick and simple, and can be sent to anyone, anywhere, anytime. But it's also very easy to ignore. You want your message to be more memorable, and only personal communication channels, such as the phone or a video chat, can achieve that. The other person will be able to actually hear and/or see that you are paying attention to them.

Attentional Networking - what should you do now?

You don't need to be a master to start building your network. Just taking a moment to reach out and give attention to another human being is a big step that will help most people. Sharing useful information and connecting like-minded people are simple actions that everyone will appreciate. It helps others and will clarify your real attention and intentions.

Attentional networking can make a huge difference if you focus on being useful, giving attention to others and don't make things harder than they have to be.

For me, Attentional Networking is a process. It's about professionalism and being persistent. This process takes place every time you meet someone. The initial contact is the highest stress point for 95% of people. Why? You are taking a huge leap of faith. It always amazes me how two strangers can become friends in a very short space of time.

I watch them meet, start to chat and, after a while, they lock in on each other and have a wonderful conversation. This is the true purpose of networking – to act as a catalyst, bringing two people together. This is the foundation for building authentic relationships.

The Art of 'Attentional Networking', in professional as well as in personal life, begins with the simple step of being genuinely interested in other people, whoever they are. Let this type of networking become your way of life. When you do that, you will start to experience many magical things: greater business results, more happiness and satisfaction, and less stress in your daily life.

Attentional Networking, or the art of building mutually beneficial relationships (rather than networking for personal gain), is the foundation of my speaking, seminar and training business.

PART FOUR

The Attention Switch

"The simple act of paying
attention can take you
a long way."

Keanu Reeves

CHAPTER 5

PAY ATTENTION AND WIN LIFE'S CHALLENGES

"The essence of all art
is to have pleasure
in giving pleasure."

Dale Carnegie

CHAPTER 5: PAY ATTENTION AND WIN LIFE'S CHALLENGES

When and where do you best connect with other people? What elements strengthen—or undermine—your ability and motivation to connect with others? These questions always bring diverse answers. Why? When dealing with people the one-size-fits-all principle doesn't work. Strategies that help you connect with others may not help your colleagues or friends; what works for your boss doesn't always work for you. When we deal with people personality matters. It is time to turn the Attention Switch ON!

THE POWER OF ATTENTION IMPROVES YOUR WEALTH

> "Not he who has much is rich,
> but he who gives much."
>
> Erich Fromm

Your ability to grow into wealth depends very much on your attention. You can have wealth, all your needs can be taken care of and so much more, if you focus your authentic attention on the right people and the right opportunities. Your authentic Attention has amazing (almost magical) power to cleanse your mind and inspire it with the right ideas. Experience this once and you will want to experience it again.

When you fix on this power of attention to others both consciously and subconsciously, you will attract new circumstances and people into your life. As I will explain in more detail in the next chapter, I believe that your attention is like a bank, a sort of borderless, non-physical financial institution. The interest on your attention deposits will lead to either wealth or poverty.

So, if you are fearful about connecting with others, you're actually attracting negative situations and people into your life. These will only create obstacles, lack and limitations and will prevent you from becoming the person you really want to be.

Whatever you deposit in your mental bank will multiply and grow: positive or negative, good or bad, abundance or lack. So you'd better put good authentic thoughts and ideas regarding others in there. These thoughts will connect you and bring you closer to other people, which by itself will attract more abundance and prosperity into your life.

If you convince yourself that giving attention to others will bring you wealth, if you are being authentic and let that authenticity attract and circulate abundance in your life – then you will always have real wealth, regardless of the form it takes, be it deeper, more long lasting relationships or more money. Or both! Your wealth is never truly dependent on cash, but it is definitely influenced by the amount of attention you invest in others.

COURAGE = PAYING ATTENTION, LIVING CONSCIOUSLY

> "Courage is
> resistance to fear,
> mastery of fear –
> not absence of fear."
>
> Mark Twain

Are fears holding you back? Are you afraid of talking to strangers? How would you live if you had no fear at all? You'd still have your intelligence and the common sense necessary to safely navigate around any real dangers, but without fear would you be more willing to take risks, especially when the worst case wouldn't actually hurt you at all?

Would you speak up more often, give your attention to more strangers? What if you even learned to enjoy the things you currently fear? What kind of difference would that make in your life?

When I talk about courage I'm not referring to the heroic kind you'd need if you risked your life saving someone from a burning building. By courage I mean the ability to face down those imaginary fears and reclaim the powerful life that you've denied yourself. Fear of being alone. Fear of failure. Fear of public speaking. Fear of rejection. Fear of speaking to strangers. Fear of going broke. Fear of physical discomfort. Fear of regret. Fear of success. Fear of being authentically YOU!

In our day-to-day lives, the virtue of courage doesn't receive much Attention, especially with regards to interactions with other people. Courage is a quality reserved for soldiers, firefighters and activists. Security is what matters most today. Perhaps you were taught to avoid being too bold or too brave. It's too dangerous! Don't take unnecessary risks. Don't draw attention to yourself in public. Follow family traditions. Don't talk to strangers. Keep an eye out for suspicious people. Stay safe.

There are real dangers that must be avoided, but a side effect of overemphasizing the importance of personal security is that it can cause you to live reactively. Instead of setting your own goals, making plans to achieve them, and going after them with gusto; you play it safe.

What is courage?

Courage is the ability to give attention and to be able to motivate yourself to take action in spite of fear.

Courageous people still feel fear, but they don't let the fear paralyze them. People who lack courage will give into fear more often than not, which has the long-term effect of strengthening the fear. The older you get, the more you will take your fears for granted; they will become real to you.

But there's something else going on in your head, right?

That tiny voice at the back of your mind recalls that this isn't the kind of life you wanted to live. It wants more, much more. And if you refuse to listen and pay real attention to it, it will always be there, nagging you about your mediocre results until the day you die, full of regrets for what might have been.

In the past, I have faced many scary moments where I have chosen to back down and take the easy route. Eventually I learned to choose a different response and, over the years, I've helped many people worldwide develop their ability to cope with fears and connect with other people with amazing success. I believe there are a few key factors that will either support or destroy your ability to embrace your inner daring. Here is what helped me.

1. Connect with your WHY

You want to choose the path that is filled with joy, right? So how do you choose between two options? Ask yourself why you would take each path. Is it because one is easier, safer, and more certain? Or is it because it sets your heart on fire, ignites your passion and calls you to become a bigger and better version of yourself? Now, try to connect with your heart.

Try to connect to your feelings when you think of the two options. You will soon get a sense which path is based on fear and which is rooted in love.

If you choose to take the more challenging path, the one that is rooted in love, remain connected to your why throughout the whole process. Remind yourself why you have made this choice. Anytime fear comes up, come back to your why. Think about all the amazing positive aspects of this new path and move forward with your beautiful end result in mind.

2. Understand your fears about approaching people

Many years of experience and reading motivational books have taught me that fear is actually a sort of self-protection. That fearful inner voice is trying to keep you safe. It wants security, stability, comfort and sameness. It does not want to see you fail, as it believes this will risk the love and acceptance it thinks you need to survive.

Just take a step back from these fearful thoughts and recognize that they are simply trying to protect you. You don't have to buy into them. Identify these thoughts and notice them. Then, all you need to do is simply say to yourself "thank you thoughts, I know you are just trying to protect me, but I am safe and all is well and only good lies before me." And then, let them go and give yourself the space to make the right decision.

3. Decide. Commit. Act

Daring doesn't thrive on too much deliberation. Take too long over making a decision and your willingness to take a bold new step could wither and die. We don't really need to take that long to make a decision. Make the decision quickly, commit yourself to it and follow through with immediate action. Remember Goethe's famous quote:

"Whatever you do, or dream you can, begin it! Boldness has genius and power and magic in it."

You must follow through with action, don't stop and think about what you are doing! If you procrastinate, wait or decide to think about it for a bit longer, you will lose your moment. When the impulse is there you must jump in immediately. If you wait, you will simply be giving your old fears the perfect opportunity to talk you out of it. Without a proactive action plan, nothing will happen.

Are you scared of talking to others? Are you freaking out at the thought of interacting with another human being? That is a good sign. It means you DARE! You are taking a leap of faith out of your comfort zone and in to the zone where dreams begin to come true.

4.   Be willing to not know

Being willing not to know how things are going to develop once you take a risk in life forces you to become extremely present and to embrace uncertainty. All you can do is take life one step at a time. Just take the step that lies before you at this very moment and do not worry about anything else.

Nobody gets all the answers all at once. They will be revealed over time. By giving your real attention to the (unknown) process and trusting it, you actually create a beautiful space for the universe to step in and help you to connect with others with authenticity.

5.   Support yourself

Do not forget to give Attention to yourself! It is important to support yourself with positive and empowering thoughts while you are expanding beyond your comfort zone. Take some quiet time and connect with your inner guidance.

Congratulate yourself on having the courage to take these steps, give yourself positive reinforcement for all the actions you take along the way. Believe in yourself at all times. Avoid listening to negative inner voices that cut you down or hold you back. Go forward with your actions to fulfill your dreams and give authentic attention to other people.

SEIZE THE MOMENT

> "It is in your moments of decision
> that your destiny is shaped."
>
> Tony Robbins

We frequently get caught up in our routines and habits and find ourselves feeling disconnected from the people around us. Or even from ourselves. Instead, we spend our time and energy thinking and dwelling on people and events from the past.

Giving authentic attention is an immediate action in the present moment. Disturbing thoughts prevent us from truly being able to engage and connect, right now, with others in our lives.

One of the suggestions in motivational literature and books on popular psychology is to attend to every moment mindfully. Mindfulness means that we pay authentic attention to everything that happens within our bodies and around us in the present moment. We do not judge it or get into an internal dialogue about it. Being mindful to other people means we need to pay attention to them without prejudice. Do not categorize or evaluate every person you meet. Learn to enjoy the experience.

By using mindfulness techniques to pay attention to others, we can begin to take more control of our relationships and interactions with other human beings. We learn to switch off the autopilot. Learning to be fully aware of our connection with others, our thoughts and emotions—whether they are pleasant or unpleasant—helps us deal with stress more effectively. It'll help us avoid giving our attention to and connecting with the wrong people.

Everyone can learn how to pay mindful attention to others. Repeatedly paying attention to one person in one moment will help you get better at connecting with others. I'm not suggesting that simply paying attention to other people is the answer to all networking and life challenges. But it is obvious that if your mind is clear you'll be able to solve life issues more easily and your connections with others will be more meaningful and successful.

PAY ATTENTION AND ADD VALUE IMMEDIATELY

> "The value of a man should be seen in what he gives and not in what he is able to receive."
>
> Albert Einstein

At its core, paying attention and connecting with others is about adding value. Adding value by paying attention builds authentic long-term relationships.

But you need to add value right from the beginning, even before you've developed a relationship with the other person.

This may seem strange and maybe even somewhat naïve. Why should you give away value to some stranger who may never want to build a relationship with you?

Try to put yourself in the shoes of the other person. Imagine that somebody you've only just met shows interest in you and sincerely gives you their attention: they listen to you, share quality time with you, and are even willing to help you. Isn't it amazing that somebody you don't know has put your interests first? Wouldn't you react positively to this person? Will you feel more comfortable with this person and feel that you can count on her? Immediately adding value to someone else, while paying attention, is a solid, fast and efficient way to build trust and convey confidence.

You need to be constantly alert to other people's needs and desires. Every time you meet another person ask yourself how you can help them. The sooner you get into help and adding value mode the faster you connect with the other person and the purer your authentic attention will be.

I like to arrive early every time I give a keynote presentation. Sometimes, I join for the whole event. Why? In the time before the session starts, I try to connect with new people. I learn how I can help them and what value they are looking for. What do I gain? When I'm on stage, I can start giving immediate value to all the people I met. Moreover, after the event, I gain new contacts that are happy to hear from me again. I gain new people who I can build authentic relationships with. Not to mention that my willingness to add value to others differentiates me from many other speakers. Thus, most of the attendees remember me for a longer time and, over the years, some of them have become close friends.

If you want to connect with others fast and effectively, then learn to add immediate value to each of them. Don't doubt them, just listen carefully for their needs and find out how you can help. You will surprise not only them but also yourself!

PAY ATTENTION AND TAKE ACTION... EVEN IF YOU MAY FAIL

"Courage and perseverance have a magical talisman, before which difficulties disappear and obstacles vanish into air."

John Quincy Adams

How many times have you been paralyzed from taking action because of your fears? What did you feel at that moment? What did you do? Did you conquer your fears or let them win? Do you pay ATTENTION to your way of reacting to fear?

Whatever your answers to these questions may be, that's okay. While diving right in and confronting a fear head-on can be very effective, it may require more courage than you feel you can summon right now.

The most important point I want you to learn is that real courage is a mental skill, not an emotional one. That skill will help you in developing your networking and relationship building skills. It's also helpful when you decide to give sincere Attention to other human beings (who might need a little courage themselves!)

You can overcome any limitation you have, including fears, and gain courage, by using your human intelligence and logic. When you learn how to do it, it feels great!

I want to share two methods with you. I've practiced them for years and I've found them very effective in boosting my courage and helping me give my sincere attention even to strangers. The two methods have helped people who are close to me too and I encourage you to use them.

Method one: progressive training

To conquer fears and gain courage, you do not need to take drastic action! We can compare building courage to weight training. Just as weight training strengthens your muscles, training that deals with fears strengthens your courage. Courage is a learned mental skill that you can condition and hone. When you start weight-training, you don't try to lift 500kg right away. Similarly, if you want to be courageous, start with a small fear and save the big ones for later.

Try the following exercise:

Step 1: Write down one of the fears that you'd like to overcome. (Yes, WRITE it, don't just think about it. Writing something down helps turn your thoughts into actions!)

Step 2: Write down ten variations of this fear.

Step 3: Go through the list and decide which is the scariest and which is the least scary. Number them accordingly, with number one being the least anxiety producing and number ten being the most anxiety producing. This is your fear hierarchy.

For example, if you're afraid of approaching a stranger at a networking event, then number one on your list might be going to an event and smiling at someone you do not know (very mild fear). Number two might be smiling at ten interesting strangers on a single day of the conference. (I mean ten people that you might approach to start a conversation with). Number ten might be asking to schedule a meeting, in front of all your friends, when you're almost certain you'll be turned down flat and everyone in the room will laugh cruelly at you (extreme fear)!

How do you begin? First, set a goal to complete number one on your list. Once you've had that success (and success in this case simply means taking action, regardless of the outcome), then move on to number two, and so on, until you're ready to tackle number ten... In no time, you will feel the fear starting to lose its grip.

Remember – make the actions on your list practical so that you can actually work through them!

What if the step is too big? Break it down into additional steps. It's exactly like weight lifting – if you can lift 490kg but not 500kg, then try 491 or even 492. The next step is a mild challenge for you; it will help you gain confidence that you can achieve the big goal. Furthermore, I advise you to repeat a past step multiple times as you will find it helps you to prepare for the next step. Pace yourself.

This method is easy to follow and it will create a progressive training process for your mental skill. Thus, I am sure that you will stop reinforcing the fear that you once had.

The fact that your feelings of fear will diminish at the same time that your courage grows will help you to act with a lot more daring in similar situations in the future. Thus, let the other person feel that you are really giving him your authentic attention. Try it and you will find it amazingly useful!

Method 2: Acquire additional knowledge and skills

This second method is especially effective when you fear the unknown. Sometimes your fear, or courage deficiency, stems from a lack of knowledge or skill. Many professionals that I know personally are great at what they do but are still very fearful and even 'hate' networking. This fear developed largely due to ignorance and lack of networking (relationship-building) skills in these professionals. A very practical way to deal with these sorts of fears is by gathering information and signing up for a training program.

For example, if you're afraid to approach people and start a conversation at a networking event even though you'd absolutely love to be more social, then start reading books and taking classes on how to use 'attention' to create relationships (you could sign up for one of my trainings or events). You could do research online or join a club, association or any relevant trade organization in your field.

Attend conferences. Build connections. Many people choose to use and enlist the help of myself as their networking and relationship mentor and coach. I would be happy to help you as well.

This knowledge will help you act more boldly and courageously when you're ready. It will enhance your confidence and instill new ideas – maybe even the idea that you really can succeed. I've proved it over and over again during events and conferences, by taking a shy person out of their comfort zone and turning them into a sincere Attention giver and relationship-builder. It takes a few minutes, that's all.

Please remember: fear is not your enemy. It is a compass pointing you to the areas where you need to grow. So when you encounter a new fear within yourself, celebrate it as an opportunity for development, just as you would celebrate reaching a new personal best in strength training.

BE PRESENT AND PAY ATTENTION TO SUCCESS

"The secret of health for both mind and body is not to mourn for the past, worry about the future, or anticipate troubles, but to live in the present moment wisely and earnestly."

Buddha

There are many ways your attention can be diverted from someone you are talking to. In fact, you probably cease paying attention to the people you are with many times during the day.

While you can physically be present and interacting with one person, you can also mentally be present at another time and place dealing with someone else. How often do you think about your loved ones when you meet somebody who reminds you of them? Or, you look at the clock and think about seeing your friend in an hour's time. These are the kinds of thoughts that divert your mind from your present activity and from the person you are supposed to be giving your attention to.

The literature says that the average person's mind wanders from some activity about 46% of the time. That also applies to when we're paying attention to other people. The total time lost during every activity, including connecting with others (sex being a possible exception), was about 30%. That's a lot of time that we don't pay real attention.

Just think how much more successful you could be in your interaction with other people if you could stop daydreaming and devote all your attention in that moment to this one person. In other words, letting your attention focus on the specific person for longer periods of time would mean a significant increase in your ability to build a relationship with that person. Paying attention to another person is a habit. Like any other habit, you need to develop your self-discipline to become more successful. One good exercise is to keep repeating these words to yourself: 'Pay Attention'. Say it silently several times while you are talking to another person. It will help you devote your attention to them and ignore any other thoughts. If I'm having a bit of an off day and can't connect with someone with as much focus as I usually can, I prefer to leave this person and connect with them at a time when I'm really able to pay attention. Otherwise, it would be unfair on them and I may miss out on a great opportunity to connect with another interesting person.

Over time, I promise you, you will learn to cut out more and more of these distracting thoughts and pay your full and sincere attention to one person. This will help you connect with people faster and with more intensity and you will achieve greater success. So, be present every moment of your time and pay attention.

GIVE ATTENTION TO THE PEOPLE YOU WANT IN YOUR LIFE

"You can have everything in life you want if you will just help enough other people get what they want."

Zig Ziglar

Are you able to give your authentic attention to the people you desire to connect with? Are you attracting the people you want into your life?

The law of attraction also works when we are dealing with attention to other people. If we give authentic attention to the people we want to connect with, to the people we want to attract into our life, we will get what we want. When that happens, you'll discover the truth of something I've been saying for many years: "If you have contacts, you don't need money". Let me give you an example.

I was participating in an event in Miami. It was evening and a group of us felt like going out. We decided to visit one of the best clubs in Miami Beach. There were only guys in our group, and we were stopped and not allowed to enter the club. I decided to wait outside while my friends went back to the hotel. I wanted to watch the crowd waiting in line to get into the party.

Suddenly I noticed a small muscular man with two blonde girls trying to enter the club through the VIP entrance. But they were also stopped and were not allowed to go in. I cannot logically explain what happened next. I approached this man and the ladies and asked them if they wanted to go inside. The man nodded. Then I said: "I will arrange it." My thoughts went into overdrive. Why did I promise them that? I couldn't get in myself!

While all these thoughts ran on, I noticed a Jewish man promoting the club. I decided to approach him. In a few seconds I found myself in an energetic and interesting conversation with this promoter. "Do you want to go in the club?" he asked. My heart was pumping hard. "Sure," I answered, feeling like God had listened to my prayers. "What about my friends?" I pointed at the man with the two ladies. "Bring them with you," the promoter answered.

Five minutes later I found myself in the club accompanied by the small man and the two ladies. It was amazing, I could not believe it. I'd done it again! The small man took me to one side: "Thank you my friend," he said while clapping on my shoulder. "What you did was amazing. My name is Rick and these are two of my dancers. I own 17 clubs in Canada and I want you to have my card." He handed me his golden business card. "You are very welcome to come to my clubs whenever you are in Canada. You will be a VIP in any of my clubs for the rest of your life." Wow!

Six months later, we had our annual international lawyer association event in Vancouver. I contacted Rick as I'd promised him. He arranged a surprise for me – he printed 200 VIP cards with my company logo so I could hand them out to my contacts and let them have fun for free in any of his clubs. He did it out of his own free will and I'm sure he'll do something similar when I next visit Canada.

It cost me nothing to get into the club in Miami, nor did it cost me anything to entertain 200 lawyers in a club in Canada; all this happened because I gave simple and authentic attention to people without any expectation of getting anything in return.

Every circumstance and every person you attract into your life is there because you gave it your attention sometime, somehow. You talked about it, you visualized it, and you remembered it. You need to give intent attention to desired people if you want to attract more success to your life. It is exactly like doing a search on Google. You need to enter the desired keywords to find the required information. It's the same with finding and connecting with the people you want.

Are you using affirmations to get to these desired people? Please be aware that a positive affirmation can have negative consequences. Affirmations do not work all the time, especially when we are dealing with attention to other people. Many times the affirmation we are told to use is not true for the specific person who says it. The fact is that if you keep telling yourself things that do not feel true for yourself, you will attract negative consequences into your life. If you try to give attention to another person by using an affirmation that is untrue, you will not be able to give an authentic attention. The small voice in your head whispers to you – 'it is not true'.

So how do you attract these desired people into your life? There are different ways you can choose to give attention to them. If you keep giving attention to what's happening and to the people who make it happen, you'll keep getting more of what's happening and you will increasingly connect with the people who make it happen. Just keep giving your desires and the desired people attention on a consistent basis and you will surely attract them into your life.

SERVE OTHERS WITH GRACE AND LOVE

> "Everybody can be great, because everybody can serve. You don't have to have a college degree to serve. You don't have to make your subject and your verb agree to serve… You only need a heart full of grace, a soul generated by love."
>
> Martin Luther King, Jr.

Why is it that most people don't know how to pay attention to others? It seems that many associate the ability to connect with other people with sales skills and most of us do not like to appear aggressive or pushy. But what if I told you that the person who is able to give authentic attention is the person who truly knows how to serve? Isn't it true that most of us like to serve other people?

Ironically your ability to give attention, your ability to care for other people, is directly related to your ability to serve them. It's a skill every person can learn and master.

Giving attention by rendering service to others will benefit your life in a few dimensions:

1.   You get to truly understand your value to other people. What problems can you help others to solve? Does your service increase their efficiency, help them build their own confidence or give them any other practical benefit? Once you understand the difference your simple service can make in other people's lives, you will never want to stop giving your attention to others.

2.   You get to learn which people you really like and who you want to have as your friend or client or partner. What challenges does your contact face? What is important to the people you want to give your attention to and how can you help them get more of that? By helping others, you get to know the problems they need to solve and how you can best help.

3.   You get to focus on solutions that work. How can you help the other person achieve his goals faster and more efficiently? How can you use your own resources to give others immediate help? Solving other people's problems by paying attention to them adds more abundance and a sense of real purpose to your life.

Each and every person that comes to you in need is an opportunity to enhance your personal happiness. Remember that by helping another, all you need to do is touch one heart and you will create a ripple of light and abundance that extends beyond the radius of that initial interaction. To serve others, you must have power. You need to have the power to forget your own concerns and worries and go out there and serve all the people who cross your path by giving them your attention. When you concentrate on helping other people solve their problems, you'll forget about yours and they will disappear.

Anyone can be great because anyone can serve! As so eloquently stated by Dr. Martin Luther King Jr., in The Drum Major Instinct sermon on February 4, 1968 in Atlanta, Georgia:

"If you want to be important – wonderful. If you want to be recognized – wonderful. If you want to be great – wonderful. But recognize that he who is greatest among you shall be your servant. That's a new definition of greatness.

"And this morning, the thing that I like about it: by giving that definition of greatness, it means that everybody can be great, because everybody can serve. You don't have to have a college degree to serve. You don't have to make your subject and your verb agree to serve. You don't have to know about Plato and Aristotle to serve. You don't have to know Einstein's theory of relativity to serve. You don't have to know the second theory of

thermodynamics in physics to serve. You only need a heart full of grace, a soul generated by love. And you can be that servant."

DO YOU PAY ATTENTION TO WINNING OR *NOT LOSING*?

"Remembering that you are going to die is the best way I know to avoid the trap of thinking you have something to lose."

Steve Jobs

Imagine you are in front of your TV and five of your favourite shows are showing at the same time (please ignore for the sake of this example that we can record and save TV programmes these days).

You want to watch all of them! You start zapping from channel to channel trying watch all the programmes at once. It's exhausting. You start to get confused and change the channels at random. You use so much energy and attention in avoiding missing the shows that you don't take the time to reconsider your options or really watch any of them.

Now imagine instead of TV programmes we are dealing with the people you want to meet. What will you do then?

Here's a word of advice – get rid of this approach toward life. Stop! Prioritise your challenges. Slow down. Work out how many people you want to approach and when and where you would like to meet them. With this in mind, your approach toward the game of life and developing relationships with others will be much more successful. You will actually have a chance to play to win instead of playing to avoid losing.

When I look back on my life, I see many life challenges. My main relationship-building challenges were: to move away from negative people and surround myself with more positive ones; to learn to pay attention to myself before giving it to others; to learn and practice networking authentically with other people.

All these relationship life challenges are a total no-brainer for me now. Do you know why? I've accomplished them all. I've had practice. If someone said to me "did you know that you need to give attention to yourself before giving your attention to others?" I would be like…"Duh." And if someone said "did you know that to be happier you need to get rid of negative people in your life?" I would be like "Well, double duh."

Over the years I've become an expert and even a global authority on some aspects of these challenges. Even though I give many keynote presentations and trainings on networking and relationship capital, I still see my skill in this area as a work in progress. In this book, you are taking the journey with me – learning from the mistakes I made and hearing some of the successes I had.

Maybe these are not the relationship and connecting challenges you are going through yourself, maybe they are far from it. Perhaps you have yet to encounter these challenges, or perhaps you have been there, done that, and are already an expert.

So I encourage you to think of your current top three life challenges with regards to relationships and connecting with other people. What are the top three issues that keep bothering you and preventing you from being a real attention giver? Give this exercise your authentic attention.

Remember that life challenges are specific and personal. The one-size-fits-all principle does not apply when we are dealing with building relationships with other people. Personality matters a great deal. Your personal attention, which is unique for every person, acts as your relationship 'finger print'.

Now, please describe the kinds of situations where you do well. You feel like a winner and are motivated and effective in these areas. Do you know what they are? Don't expect to get just one answer to this question. Now have a look at both sets of answers. Can you see the difference between answering questions from a winner's viewpoint and from the perspective of someone who really doesn't want to lose?

I want to help you predict your performance. When you know and understand your current level of attention, you will be able to use it better and create much more successful results.

In business the most common tool for identifying one's personality type is the Myers-Briggs Type Indicator. But this indicator does not claim to predict performance. Fortunately, there is a way and it's used by psychologists and marketing research companies.

This system groups people into types on the basis of a personality attribute that predicts performance. According to this system there are two types of people (I'll use my own terminology to make a direct connection to the subject of this book):

(1) **Promotion Attention people;**

(2) **Prevention Attention people.**

Promotion Attention people focus on the rewards they will get or achieve; they will create a path to lead them to that achievement. They pay attention to winning. Their attention giving ability affects how they approach life's challenges and demands. They will take chances by giving attention to strangers, dreaming big dreams, being creative and trying to connect quickly with others.

These people are willing to pay a price for the errors they make along the way to developing solid relationships, since the worst that can happen is missing a chance to meet a new person, or failing to progress a relationship.

Prevention Attention people, in contrast, concentrate on staying safe. They worry about connecting with the wrong people or about not preparing enough. They are vigilant and pay attention to not losing as they want to maintain the status quo. These people aren't usually the ones who look to connect with others in more creative ways.

You're probably already trying to guess which category you belong to. First, we are all promotion and prevention attention people at different times and in different circumstances. But most of us have a dominant motivational attention. This attention affects who you pay attention to, who you value, and how you feel when you succeed or fail in giving your attention to another person.

So go and give your attention to winning, NOW!

ATTENTION RELIEVES STRESS

"The greatest gift you can give another is the purity of your attention."

Richard Moss

Here's a simple solution to stress. It's been used for centuries as a golden key to a good life. I'm sharing it here because you deserve this gift!

Focused attention instantly stills emotions. Thus, mind control is possible. Ask yourself the following questions: "what am I thinking?" and "what do I feel?" These questions help you become self-aware. Self-awareness prompts your mind to respond to these questions. It will give you the power to cope with challenges in your life. Now add the attention ingredient to it and the game has changed. Focus your attention on the emotions that enter your mind and get familiar with them. By recognizing and accepting the emotions, you prevent them from running wild in your mind and causing stress. This takes some practice, but over time you will learn how to calm your more troubling emotions.

It's one of the deepest powers of attention and you can give it to yourself and to other people. It has a powerful and magical effect, as you will see for yourself.

The Indian Maharajah

On one of my trips to Kiev, Ukraine, I was joined by a pleasant young colleague. He's funny, not so tall and of Hindu origin. I used to have fun with him and called him the Indian Maharajah.

On one of our trips, I felt that my colleague was not his usual self... It was as though he wanted to share something with me but did not know where to start. As we had quite a lot of time together during the trip, I let him open up. What I heard was amazing.

It turned out that my colleague and his wife had been trying to have children for several years but with no success. They went through all sorts of treatments but nothing really helped. As my colleague was a practicing Hindu, he approached his guru for advice.

My colleague told me: "The guru said to me – 'do not try too hard. You will soon meet a very special good person and you will get close to him. You should enjoy every moment. This joy and goodness is your solution'."

The guru continued and explained to my colleague that the meeting with this person would help release all the difficulties of trying to get a baby.

My colleague looked at me: "This was nine months ago..." His eyes filled with tears. "You and I met during that period. Now my wife is pregnant and about to deliver a baby boy."

My heart felt as though it would overflow.

"You are the one my guru was talking about. You brought us the good inspiration and real happiness we were missing. We would like to give back to you. We want to name our new baby boy after you, Itzik."

I felt like I was dreaming. I could not believe it was the truth.

We both sank into each other arms for a big sincere hug. I really learned the power of authentic attention and winning one of the life's greatest challenges. I will never forget it. I will cherish this memory for the rest of my life.

DIRECT YOUR ATTENTION

> "The ego is nothing other than the focus of conscious attention."
>
> Alan Watts

During the research for this book I found that one scholar compares 'Attention' to a flashlight. Like a flashlight, we should use attention to cast light on a single item. We should shine our attention on a single person so that we can see them more clearly.

But have you ever tried aiming a flashlight on one object for a long period of time? During my army days, we once had to hold a huge projector and aim it constantly on the path ahead so we could see at night. It was difficult! It is even harder to aim the attention beam on just one person.

Let's take another step. What happens if you direct that attention on yourself – 'self-focused attention'? In this case, you'll create an endless loop of thoughts that may beget worries, sadness, and anxiety. Do you recognize this situation in your life? I am sure you do. As an aside, this also causes the fear of public speaking that so many people suffer from.

Psychology researchers Nilly Mor, PhD, and Jennifer Winquist, PhD, confirmed those findings in their 2002 study that linked self-focused attention with depression, anxiety and negative moods.

When you direct your attention inward, you will be less capable of enjoying your life and appreciating your surroundings. Your attention is no longer in the present with the people you are with. This can lead to feelings of distress, depression and anxiety. The right direction to direct your attention is outside, toward other people.

So what can you do to direct your attention and win life challenges? First, recognize the obstacles that prevent you from focusing your attention. For example, avoid external media and social media disturbance. Second, learn to focus your attention on the right people, the ones who are presently part of your life, and try to develop authentic relationships with them.

You should go out there and invest in your attention skills and relationship-building abilities, for example by reading this book again. This is one of the best investments you can make in yourself and it will pay dividends in all aspects of your life. People around you will come to life the moment you give them your attention. And there's no time like the present to get started.

I am not sure if you are familiar with the following story (from an unknown source) but it is a great example of how important it is to direct your attention while dealing with life challenges. Read and draw your own conclusions.

The hospital

Two men, both seriously ill, occupied the same hospital room. One man was allowed to sit up in his bed for an hour each afternoon to help drain the fluid from his lungs. His bed was next to the room's only window. The other man had to spend all his time flat on his back.

The men talked for hours on end. They spoke of their wives and families, their homes, their jobs, their military service, and where they had been on vacation. And every afternoon when the man in the bed by the window could sit up, he would pass the time by describing to his room mate all the things he could see outside. The man in the other bed began to live for those one-hour periods where his world would be broadened and enlivened by all the activity and colour of the outside world.

The window overlooked a park with a lovely lake, the man said. Ducks and swans played on the water while children sailed their model boats. Lovers walked arm in arm amid flowers of every colour of the rainbow. Grand old trees graced the landscape, and a fine view of the city skyline could be seen in the distance. As the man by the window described all this in exquisite detail, the man on the other side of the room would close his eyes and imagine the picturesque scene.

One warm afternoon the man by the window described a parade passing by. Although the other man couldn't hear the band, he could see it in his mind's eye as the gentleman by the window portrayed it with descriptive words. Unexpectedly, an alien thought entered his head: why should he have all the pleasure of seeing everything while I never get to see anything? It didn't seem fair. As the thought fermented the man felt ashamed at first. But as the days passed and he missed seeing more sights, his envy became resentment and soon turned him sour. He began to brood and he found himself unable to sleep. He should be by that window – that thought now controlled his life.

Late one night as he lay staring at the ceiling, the man by the window began to cough. He was choking on the fluid in his lungs. The other man watched in the dimly lit room as the struggling man by the window groped for the button to call for help. Listening from across the room he never moved, never pushed his own button, which would have brought the nurse running. In less than five minutes the coughing and choking stopped, along with the sound of breathing. Now there was only silence – deathly silence.

The following morning the day nurse arrived to bring water for their baths. When she found the lifeless body of the man by the window, she was saddened and called the hospital attendants to take it away. As soon as it seemed appropriate, the other man asked if he could be moved next to the window. The nurse was happy to make the switch, and after making sure he was comfortable, she left him alone.

Slowly, painfully, he propped himself up on one elbow to take his first look. Finally, he would have the joy of seeing it all himself. He strained to slowly turn to look out the window beside the bed.

It faced a blank wall.

"Do just once
what others say you can't do,
and you will never
pay attention
to their limitations again."

James Cook

CHAPTER 6

HOW TO ENHANCE YOUR PAYING ATTENTION SKILLS

"The simple act of
paying positive attention
to people has a great deal
to do with productivity."

Tom Peters

CHAPTER 6: HOW TO ENHANCE YOUR PAYING ATTENTION SKILLS

Every time I speak with somebody, I know it is another great opportunity to practice my attention skills. When I'm unsure whether I'm spending time with the 'right' person, I will pay extra special attention and decide if what the other person tells me make sense.

Knowing how to pay attention is just as important in your personal life as it is in your professional career. You have to learn how to pay attention to other people if you want to move forward in any aspect of your life.

Only a few of us are born with well developed attention giving skills. Most of us need to practice our networking and relationship-building abilities, and that's why it's so important to develop the fundamental skill of giving attention.

Paying attention should be taught and practiced, and I am always looking for new teaching techniques for these vital skills. I am sure you agree with me that just because you have two ears on the side of your head doesn't mean you automatically know how to pay real and authentic attention.
I want you to practice tuning in, not tuning out from people.

HOW MUCH DO YOU WANT WHAT YOU WANT?

"Desire is the starting point of all achievement, not a hope, not a wish, but a keen pulsating desire which transcends everything."

Napoleon Hill

Did you ever check how much you really want what you want in your life? How much do you want more success in your life? How much do you want more happiness in your life? How much do you really want to connect with other people and build relationships with them? Do you want to have it as badly as you want air when your head is underwater (like the famous story about Socrates and the young man)?

It helps to make these three commitments to yourself, specifically with regards to giving attention to others:

• **Commitment 1:** You are convinced that there is a way. You are determined to find a way to leave the things that bother you behind, especially poor communication and unsatisfactory relationships.

• **Commitment 2**: You have a sincere and strong desire to overcome the challenges in your life, specifically the challenge to authentically connect with others.

• **Commitment 3:** You've decided to follow your own path, specifically to give more of your attention to others, to connect and build relationships.

If you do that, your success is guaranteed. You will wake inner power that will help you achieve your goals. Identify your thoughts, wants and desires with respect to connecting with other people and align those desires with your overall aim in life (whether it is a more peaceful life, a life surrounded by friends and people you love, or a life of giving to others). This will ensure you sharpen your attention skills.

THREE MAGIC ATTENTION LEVELS

> "Real magic in relationships means an absence of judgment of others."
>
> Dr Wayne Dyer

I developed the following easy method to improve attention levels during one of my international speaking engagements. I needed to come up with three practical action points that people could easily learn and implement immediately to significantly improve their attention skills. So I am proud to share it here with you my dear reader:

Level 1: Relax. Let your mind become still. Pay attention to nothing. Be peaceful with yourself.

Level 2: Choose a phrase that encapsulates how you want to relate to others. For example: "I accept all people, let them enter and bring magic into my life". Repeat this phrase for five minutes. You can choose to repeat it out loud (in front of the mirror for example) and watch your lips form every word just as your mind does. Notice how your emotions have changed after you've been repeating it for a while, or maybe you'll notice that you feel something physically.

Level 3: Close your eyes and picture a very important person coming toward you, shaking your hand and congratulating you for achieving whatever you wanted to achieve. Make this picture as vivid and detailed as possible. Play it over and over in your mind until it feels more like a memory of a real event rather than a product of your imagination.

I practice these three levels just before I go to sleep. As a result I sleep more deeply, I'm more peaceful and every morning I wake up with new hopes and fresh ideas. If you follow it properly this simple exercise will improve your life and the way you connect with others!

DO THE THING YOU FEAR

> "Do the thing you are afraid to do,
> and the death of fear is certain."
>
> Ralph Waldo Emerson

Believe it or not, but some years ago I was terrible at starting conversations with strangers. I sweated, got 'cold feet' and didn't dare say a word. My fears were literally paralyzing me. Does this sound familiar to you?

If I had given way to this fear, horrible as it was, I am sure I would never have become a global authority on networking and relationship capital and you definitely would not be reading this book. So what happened?

Michael Jackson sings these lines in 'Mirror': "I'm starting with the man in the mirror, I'm asking him to change his ways. And no message could have been any clearer. If you wanna make the world a better place, take a look at yourself and then make a change."

I made a change inside. I went to strangers and started talking to them until gradually I began enjoying it. I started discovering amazing people. I started enjoying my conversations with others. I did the thing I was afraid to do, and guess what – the fear was gone!

USE YOUR ATTENTION WISELY

> "One reason so few of us achieve what we truly want is that we never direct our focus; we never concentrate our power. Most people dabble their way through life, never deciding to master anything in particular."
>
> Tony Robbins

Now that you are aware of the power of your natural ability to give attention to others, please choose to use it wisely. Let me share some tips that help me use my attention prudently every day. By following these hints, those who get my authentic attention know that it is unique and valuable.

1. Control yourself

Work out how and when you decide to give your attention to somebody. Why do you decide to do so? And how do you really give your attention to others? My experience has taught me that many people do not control their attention giving skills and any person who wants can 'take', 'get' or 'grab' it. No wonder so many of us are uninspired by the thought of connecting with other people! Make a habit of checking your own behaviour and you will be able to control your attention more strictly and use it more efficiently.

2. Stop giving attention to negative people RIGHT NOW!

It's also important to know how to avoid giving attention to negative people. Giving your sincere attention to this sort of person will drain your energy and may even lead to stress in other relationships. Stop giving any sort of attention to these people immediately! Remember: where your attention goes your energy flows.

### 3.	In between attention

Somebody once asked me what I did in between giving attention to one person and another. "I sleep," I replied. But seriously, there are empty times before you meet another person. For example, you are standing alone at a party because you haven't decided who to talk to yet. What can you do to sharpen your attention in these moments? How do you avoid negative thoughts and feed the positive impulse that drives your attention? One simple suggestion – fill these times with good things. For example, look at some photos on your phone that bring sweet memories to mind; read a positive quote. Use anything that will help you to feel positively stronger.

### 4.	The attention 'bucket'

Your attention 'bucket' should always be whole. No damage, no leaks, no rust. In other words, no interruptions or distractions should be allowed to shift your sincere attention away from one person to another. That can create real damage. You need a complete attention 'bucket' to preserve and gather enough attention to give to other people.

### 5.	Attention 80-20 rule

Does the 80-20 rule work with attention giving? I don't have a fixed opinion about that. It is indeed true that the attention you give to 20% of the people will generate 80% of the results. But how do you know who the magic 20% will be? I don't like the idea of using some sort of selection criteria because I believe it does not exist. One suggestion – every time you give your attention to somebody, learn from it and sharpen your instinct for a similar future situation.

### 6.	Know when to stop

Always be aware of the return you currently get from your attention to other people, be it personal or professional, and stop if it's not working out well for you.

SEVEN RULES FOR GIVING ATTENTION SUCCESSFULLY

> "Motivation is what gets you started.
> Habit is what keeps you going."
>
> Jim Rohn

Let me give seven golden rules to help you when you are giving attention to others. They are based on the success rules written by Napoleon Hill.

1.   Give positive attention all the time

Give your authentic positive attention to other people all the time. Do not get annoyed or change the quality of your attention only because the other person is grumpy or negative.

2.   There are three sorts of attention in each encounter with another person

Remember there are always three sorts of attention in any encounter with another person. First, there is the attention you give to them, second there is the other person's attention for you and third, there is the right attention. The last one is the attention given by the universe to the two of you. So do not assume in every meeting that the other person is at fault if they do not give you their full attention. The chances are that if attention is not given by both parties, then both are partly to blame.

3.   Do not give attention when you are angry

If you want to be a successful relationship-builder, avoid giving your attention to others when you are angry. This emotional state will prevent you from giving sincere positive attention, even if you really want to.

4. When you give others your attention treat them as if they are royalty

Imagine you're meeting a king or a queen; what kind of attention would you give them? Positive respectful attention, right? You'll hardly dare speak and you'll listen to every word with full attention and empathy. Treat every person you meet as though they're royalty and give them some damn good attention. They deserve it... and so do you!

5. Authentic attention is about asking questions

Asking questions, as you learned earlier in the book, is an important way to show your sincere interest in other people. If somebody says something you do not understand, learn to ask: "how do you know?"

According to Napoleon Hill, it's the killer question that can lead you to success. Now wait for the other person to reply. If they are insincere you will see them struggling to find an answer.

6. Be sensitive to other people's feelings

Giving attention to another is a very powerful act. If the other person doesn't know you, they may find this act of sincere attention confusing or even slightly intimidating. Watch their reactions – pay attention – and back off if they seem even a little uncomfortable.

7. Friendly analysis attention or unfriendly criticism attention

You need to make a choice between giving friendly analysis attention or unfriendly criticism attention. What is the difference? Most people accept friendly analysis. They can learn from it and enjoy the attention you're giving them. On the other hand, most of us resent unfriendly criticism.

How do people know what kind of attention you're giving them? First, they know from the relationship they already have with you if you mean to give friendly or unfriendly attention. They can also learn it from the tone of voice and the manner in which the attention is given. Accordingly they can decide to accept and embrace it or deny and reject it.

FIVE TIPS FOR SHY PEOPLE

> "He who is not courageous enough to take risks will accomplish nothing in life."
>
> Muhammad Ali

You really want to improve your attention giving skills but.... you are shy! I've had many requests from 'shy' people for a simple way to get through their timidity so that they can give genuine attention to others.

So I decided to recap some of the ideas I've already shared and add in some of Dale Carnegie's basic techniques. These five steps work magically for everyone, especially shy people.

1.   Smile!

A smile is the ticket to everyone's heart. It is a simple, basic gesture, yet people just don't remember to do it. People are more likely to warm to someone with a broad smile on his face than they are to someone with a grim expression.

Smiles can go a long way. Ron Gutman reviewed studies about smiling and found that a smile can predict how long you will live. British researchers have found that one smile can provide the same level of brain stimulation as up to 2,000 chocolate bars. Smiling is also contagious, especially when you combine it with sincere attention.

Always remember this basic rule of attentional networking – smile!

2.   Listen.

One of the most under-appreciated Attentional networking skills that you can easily master is the ability to listen. To get people excited about you and your business you need to do more listening and less talking. Good listening is active not passive.

How many times have you walked away from a conversation with someone and couldn't remember a word they'd said? It is easy to 'zone out' and drift into your own thoughts, particularly if you are busy or bored. Yet you should be fully engaged when you are listening. That means you not only hear and understand what has been said but you have a sense of who the person is, what their passions and experiences are, and what really makes them tick.

One of the most important points Carnegie made in 'How to Win Friends and Influence People' was that people love to talk about themselves.

If you can get people to discuss their experiences and opinions—while listening with sincere interest and giving real attention—you can have a great conversation with someone without having to say much at all.

3.   Ask a question.

Asking the right questions can build trust and open lines of safe communication. Keep questions positive and focused. The right questions put the other person in the spotlight as well as building your credibility. For the shy person, it's a much smarter and easier way to engage.

The best question to ask when networking is one that shifts the focus of the conversation from you to the other person. Then you know you're giving your full attention to the other person and his needs. One example could be "If I could introduce you to your ideal new contact who would you choose?"

4.   Learn and use their first name.

I often paraphrase one of Carnegie's basic principles: someone's name is the sweetest sound to that person. You make a lasting impression when you can recall the name of someone you've met previously. How did you feel the last time someone surprised you by recalling your name?

Making the effort to learn names goes a long way toward making your interactions more memorable. Put some effort into this skill and improve the lasting impression that you make in the eyes of your new contact.

5.   Become genuinely interested in other people.

The only connections that work will be the ones that you truly care about. If you don't have a genuine interest in someone, then stop trying to connect with them. It's nearly impossible to genuinely offer help if you don't pay authentic attention. I mean real attention, not just a surface interest in what business they're in or what kind of services or products they sell! Invest genuine time in learning what really matters to them and how you can help. Learn about their background and passions.

Be genuinely helpful. You'd be surprised how rarely the simplest things get done. Being authentic in the attention you give to others isn't as hard as some may think!

If you want to learn how to become genuinely interested in other people, you should first stay true to yourself. Be yourself! Fake feelings never got anybody anywhere in the long run.

HAVE FUN AND GIVE ATTENTION!

> "People rarely succeed unless they have fun in what they are doing."
>
> Dale Carnegie

Are you confused by all the information I've shared with you? Don't worry! I know I've covered a lot of ideas, strategies and tips on how to use attention to build relationships and connect effectively. Your job is to enjoy the process and really have fun when giving attention to others.

Turning a stranger into a real contact depends so much on your desire to give authentic attention all the time.

Do you agree that you can recognize a person who enjoys connecting with others by the happy look on her face? Their happy attitude also makes you happy and they have a special energy that attracts you to them. Do you want to feel the same way? Then follow these simple suggestions.

1.   Relax and focus.

You can't be good at everything right away. Start by relaxing and focus on what you are good at already. Take the time to learn what you do not know. Focus on positive interactions with people and learn from your mistakes. Give your attention for the sake of connecting and being a nice, caring human being. The rest will take care of itself.

2.   Be happy from the inside out.

Learn to be happy all the time. Start from within and then express it on the outside with a big wide smile, a warm handshake, and the empathic way you speak and listen to others.

Reward yourself for your successes, whether they're big or small. Keep going and you'll soon grow to love meeting other people.

3.   Laugh and enjoy.

Find any opportunity you can to laugh and enjoy life's fun moments. Spend time with people who make you laugh. Laughter is contagious and a very good way to connect with others. Try it for yourself – you may be surprised.

I hope that by now you understand that connecting with others and building relationships should be fun and joyful. It is absolutely not a pushy or negative process although it may seem that way to a lot of people. It consumes a lot of energy, especially when you are authentic and sincere, but it is worth paying the price because it is such a rewarding process.

If you want to connect with others by using your natural power of attention, then you need to relax, enjoy and have great fun! Then your success will be guaranteed!

EMBRACE THE POWER OF ATTENTION

"Concentrated attention is the collection of units of power on a chosen point of intention."

James Arthur Ray

The whole subject of authentic attention fascinates me, which is why I wrote this book. I find that giving attention brings incredible rewards. Hopefully you will soon discover this for yourself.

It is one of the most important and useful skills you can acquire. This skill will let you connect authentically with others, make more real friends, and attract more clients to work with you. It is the skill that will help you achieve more in your life.

It took me a long time to understand that this was the main driver of my success. Since then, I am always searching for new ideas and ways to improve so I can become even more authentic (yes, it is possible!)

So to understand and embrace the power of (giving) attention, let me share some more tips with you. These will help you focus.

1.   Attention needs work: You need to be committed, have discipline and work hard at improving your skills.

2.   Attention needs persistence: You need to persist until you start seeing the results of your hard work. You won't necessarily get results right away. But once you master the skill, it will begin to work like magic!

3.   Attention needs clarity: Be very clear about what are you trying to achieve in giving your attention to another person. Clarity will strengthen your skills and make the attention itself clear and sharp.

4.   Attention needs to have targets: Set short-term and long-term targets for your attention giving. Thus, you will be able to measure your success and improvements over time.

5.   Attention needs to welcome change: As with everything else in life your attention should change and grow. You need to adjust your thinking and control the attention you give to others. So if, for example, you need to change the attention you're giving to a specific person you can do it immediately, achieve better results and more rewarding relationships.

"Curiosity is as much
the parent of attention,
as attention is
of memory."

Richard Whately

PART FIVE

The Last Word

"The purpose of human life
is to serve,
and to show compassion
and the will to help others."

Albert Schweitzer

CHAPTER 7

ATTENTION THEY DESERVE!

"Successful people
are always looking for
opportunities to help others.
Unsuccessful people
are always asking,
'What's in it for me?'"

Brian Tracy

CHAPTER 7: ATTENTION THEY DESERVE!

What does it really take to connect with others and give them your authentic attention? This story will illustrate many of the points I've covered in this book.

The Romanian lady

You know by now that I travel all round the world for my work. Last year I was in Bucharest, Romania which is a city that blends the old and the new in a unique way. I was there to give a keynote presentation at the annual meeting of a leading global association of accountants. I'd arranged to spend two days in meetings with local companies and two days at the conference.

I usually stay at boutique hotels or in well-known hotel chains. On this trip I was lucky to stay in a very special boutique hotel in the centre of Bucharest. It only has 18 rooms and many of the guests are celebrities or Arabian sheikhs (I learned this from the souvenirs in the glass closet in the lobby). Every room looked like a plush museum with many beautiful and authentic pieces.

I was curious about my temporary home, so I was lucky when a pretty young lady with big green eyes and warm happy smile welcomed me. Her name was Cristina; she was in charge of the hotel's guest relationships. I checked in and within an hour I was sitting with Cristina learning about this hotel's fascinating history and its previous owners.

I had to break the story to attend a meeting, but when I got back Cristina was there waiting to share the rest of it with me. After a while the owner of the hotel and his wife and son joined our discussion. I felt like I was visiting a family and sharing and celebrating with them.

All through our talk, I thought I noticed some sadness in Cristina's eyes. I didn't know what was causing it, but I felt that this lady had so much untapped power, ambition and ability. Maybe her dreams were still waiting to be fulfilled. I decided to invest some time in listening to see if I could help Cristina.

She was a really great storyteller. After talking for a while she admitted that she was a little sad and confused; she went on to tell me about her deep interest in people's behaviour. She wanted to continue her studies and focus on psychology, but she was afraid. She was unsure of herself. Maybe somehow she was resisting her greatest dreams. I made up my mind to help her change this. I talked to her and shared some ideas with her. I listened. I invited her to be my personal guest at my presentation the next day. I was not sure if she would come. To my great surprise, even though it was her day off, Cristina kept her promise and joined me. She liked it a lot. I could see a change happening within her; her eyes were starting to sparkle.

Two months later, I received a surprise email from Cristina. I quote it here with her permission. "I am writing you today because you are just about to become my essay (application form) superstar! As I told you, I am planning to study Psychology at IIT Chicago (Illinois Institute of Technology). And writing my essay about how I am going to become a positive contributor to the world, I've remembered you and our long and nice conversations, which helped and motivated me a lot! So basically, I am going to write about you being my role model." Cristina had decided to apply for postgraduate studies at Chicago University. Wow!

I quote from her essay:

"At our hotel I had a very special guest who impressed me deeply. Being a lawyer, when he felt his job did not bring enough satisfaction, he reoriented professionally. He became an international public speaker. An inspiring, famous and exceptional one.

"During many hours of conversation, he explained to me how his new profession had changed his life. With shining eyes, he told me about how much he loves working with and for people. Trying to know them as they really are, and guiding them when help was asked for on various topics: cultural, social, professional.

"I had the luck of participating at one of his seminars, 'The art of networking'. Watching him on stage I realized that there he feels really happy. He lives for his audience, is 100% dedicated to them and is ready to listen, to empathize, to give unconditional help. He has a natural ability to perform at such a high level since he is a fine connoisseur of human nature, a great psychologist, who observes, researches, draws conclusions and then is ready to excel and inspire people around him.

"I wish to meet more people like him. People who have a strong belief that involves all of their heart, not only their brain. These people are as a mirror for me: I look in their eyes and see myself in different ways. That is how I am able to know and understand myself better in various situations, through other eyes, becoming more and more valuable for those around me and being able to change something in the world. A person, an environment, a way of thinking.

"Mr. Itzik Amiel, my guest, taught me about the importance of the 'art of listening'...I believe we should begin to pay attention to everyone who is talking to us. A friend, a member of the family, colleague, business partner or even someone unknown. Sometimes, people do not talk with words. They are talking with their hearts and eyes, ashamed or afraid to bother us. We do not have to wait until someone is crying for help. We should be able to take a break from our own life and listen to others from time to time. See if and how we can help them. Often, just by listening we are giving huge help. Just by listening we may save lives and souls. We may help people to feel more confident, more powerful. We can bring hope."

I refused to believe that another human being wrote these special things about me. I had only been myself. I only wanted to pay my authentic attention to a person who had taken such great care of me. But apparently it had been a transformative experience for her. This simple attention helped Cristina crystallise her own dreams and inspired her to make them into her new reality.

January 2014. A normal email from Cristina just keeping in touch…she surprised me, big time. Her email read:

"I am in Chicago now, since three weeks ago. I've started school and it seems to be very interesting and extremely challenging. This email is just for you to know that you inspired me and my decisions. Often I am thinking of you as being a role model for me. Take good care of your gift."

Cristina made her dream come true! She is a real hero. Imagine what would have happened if I'd stayed in a different hotel that time in Romania.

Now Cristina and I are planning to hold some workshops and trainings at Chicago University to teach others the power of authentic Attention and the art of connecting with another human being. Who knows who will next make his or her dream come true by encountering us?

Last words

Connecting with people and building relationships is probably one of the most important challenges you face in life. You need to build relationships in your personal life as well as your professional life. Our success is very much based on our communication skills with other people.

Even if you have spent the past few years looking out of the window or staring at your computer screen, you must have noticed the way the world is changing. And of course we can expect many more changes to come in the future. Giving your attention to only one person becomes increasingly difficult as a lot of new distractions take up more and more of our daily lives. It's a challenge that's growing day by day.

ATTENTIONAL NETWORKER SELF-ASSESSMENT

"The power to direct
our focus on one thing
and ignore others
lies at the core of willpower."

Daniel Goleman

ATTENTIONAL NETWORKER SELF-ASSESSMENT

Are you an attention giver or attention getter? Attention is a neutral resource that every person uses in his day-to-day life, including you. It would be interesting for you to measure your current attention status and learn how to become a better attention giver so you can improve your connecting skills with other people.

The higher your current attention giving skills, the greater your chances to connect with others, be happy, and surround yourself with people you like and trust.

Please work through the self-assessment exercise below to learn a bit more about yourself. Be sincere, authentic and honest with yourself. Only you will see it!

It would be useful to do the same assessment six months from now. If you continue working to improve your attention skills, you will score higher as attention giver.

Bearing this in mind, I have tried to develop timeless ideas and solutions for attentional networking that will become increasingly relevant. Solid, insightful information and innovative action points that every person can implement successfully. The principles of authentic attention are part of human nature, and you need to practice them on a daily basis to make them into habits that support you. Try them with friends, family members, clients and even strangers. Go surprise yourself and see the amazing immediate results.

All it takes is making a choice, committing to that choice, consistently following up, improving your communication with other people, developing a real concern for others' needs and some creativity in your interaction with others.

As I sat for long hours writing this book, you were always in my mind. I could see you listening to me, sometimes responding to what I was saying, sometimes disagreeing with me. I imagined sometimes you laughed or reflected on a new thought. But what moved me more than all this is the fact that you gave me your authentic attention.

There are so many more things I wanted to tell you and share with you, my dear friend, and I will try to add at least some of them in the limited edition of this book. But if in our time together, I've inspired you to think again about the process of connecting with other people and you've started trying out some new ways to build relationships with others using your personal attention, then I have achieved what I set out to do.

So take the words of this book to heart, make a change in this world and go out there and give your authentic attention to other people. Now, it's your turn.

PART I

Please tick the statement that is true for you.

0= Never   2=Rarely   5=Occasionally   7=Often   10=All the time

The Statement	0	2	5	7	10
1. When I see a stranger, I automatically smile					
2. I offer help to others even if they did not ask for it					
3. In a meeting, I ask a lot of questions					
4. In a meeting, I always stay positive and warmhearted					
5. Authenticity is very important in my communication with others					
6. Other people's needs are important to me and I try to help and fulfil them					
7. It is important to me to be likeable and trustworthy to others					
8. I keep a positive attitude in my interaction with others					
9. I remember people's first names and use them in my interaction with them					
10. I try all kinds of innovative ways to follow up with people I meet					
Total Score (add the value of every row together)					

PART II

Please tick the statement that is true for you.

0= Never   2=Rarely   5=Occasionally   7=Often   10=All the time

The Statement	0	2	5	7	10
1. When I speak to another person, I tell them a lot about myself					
2. I want others to listen to my needs and help me					
3. I post about myself and/or my business on social media					
4. I try to get people to follow my way					
5. I connect only with people who can help my professional and personal growth					
6. I make sure people remember my name and my activities					
7. I connect only with people who have similar tastes to me					
8. It is important that people show interest in me					
9. In my conversation with others, I talk more than I listen					
10. I do not have a lot of patience for other people					
Total Score (add the value of every row together)					

PART III

Part I Total Score = ... (insert your score from table I here) = Your Attention Giving Score.

Part II Total Score = ... (insert your score from table II here) = Your Attention Getting Score.

Are you more attention giver or attention getter?

Part I – [minus] Part II = ...

RESULTS

80-100:   Congratulations! You are genuinely an Attention Giver.

50-79:   You need to improve your giving attention skills.

0-49:   You have the right approach toward life but need to learn the secrets of attention giving.

(-50) - 0:   You need to dramatically improve your attention giving skills.

(-50) - (-70):   You have a big need to get attention and not to give attention.

(-80) - (-100):   You are an Attention Getter.

"How wonderful it is
that nobody need to wait
a single moment
before starting to improve
the world."

Anne Frank

POWER NETWORKING

i-ZiK is a strategic consulting, professional development and training firm specialising in expansion and growth through empowered relationships and Attentional Networking™ with employees, customers and partners.

Our global training and mentoring company is dedicated to using authentic tools to help:

> Leaders persuade and influence others with confidence and purpose
> People enhance their networking skills by using Attentional Networking™
> Companies stand out from their rivals, attract clients and expand to new markets
> Organisations engage and motivate their employees

The customisation, implementation and necessary reviews of the training and/or mentoring program we design for you will enable behavioural change and an immediate positive impact on your business outcomes.

SERVICES

Developing Strategy
Design business development, building relationships, marketing solutions and support implementations to accelerate growth.

Enhancing Skills
Focus on developing skills needed to change behaviours, grow business, attract new clients and develop attentional leadership™.

Installing Culture

Strengthen and align the internal networking and relationships within organisations to improve and nurture collective success.

Discovering Brand

Discover, define and develop organisations' and individuals' brands and likeability to expand relationships and gain influence.

To find out how i-ZiK can help you and your organisation or to discuss speaking or training engagements, please write to: **info@itzikamiel.com**

Get your free subscription to Itzik Amiel's ongoing secrets to success at:
www.ItzikAmiel.com

Printed in Great Britain
by Amazon